DELIGHTFUL

Brazilian

COOKING

Cover Design and Illustrations by: Martine Richards Fabrizio
Cover Photo by: Chris Sollart, Technigraphic Systems, Inc.
Design, Typesetting and Production by: Celso I. Gálvez
Editor: Donald R. Bissonnette
Printed by: Publisher Press - Salt Lake City, Utah

Published by:
Ambrosia Publications
9548 Phinney Avenue North
Seattle, Washington 98103
Phone (206) 789-3693
Fax (206) 789-3693

DELIGHTFUL
Brazilian
COOKING

by Eng Tie Ang

Published by:

AMBROSIA PUBLICATIONS

Seattle, Washington

Ambrosia Publications
P.O. Box 30818
Seattle, WA 98103
Phone (206) 789-3693
Fax (206) 789-3693

Printed in the United States of America
First Edition
First Printing - August 1993

ISBN: 0-9627810-2-9

Library of Congress Catalog Number: 93-90280

Dedication

Affectionately dedicated to Inez C. Bissonnette, my mother-in-law, who passed away in July 1992 after a lifetime of helping people and bringing joy to whoever crossed her path. And to Rosanne L. Riley, her daughter, who is basically a chip off the old block.

On The Cover
Feijoada Completa

1. Brazilian Black Beans (Beans and Meats), p. 127
2. Sliced Oranges
3. Manioc Meal with Butter and Eggs, p. 18
4. Vinaigrette Sauce, p. 20
5. Collard Greens, p. 66
6. Brazilian Rice, p. 124
7. Cachaça (Brazilian Spirits) Cocktail, p. 160

Table of Contents

Acknowledgements

I would like to thank many people for their help, support and encouragement in putting this book together. First, I would like to thank those who helped in the editing process: Sara Baldwin, Goldie Caughlan, Rubens A. and Dulce Ribeiro Sigelmann, and Debbie Turner. I especially owe these people my gratitude for the arduous task of debugging my manuscript and suggesting changes. Second, for their generously allowing me to use various items for and suggestions on the cover photo, I would like to express my appreciation to: Sara Baldwin, Douglas and Ramona Delgado, Veleda Furtado, Dulce Ribeiro Sigelmann, Lynn Tungseth, as well as the following Seattle area businesses: Cascioppo Brothers, Keeg's, Nature's Elegance, Puget Consumers' Co-op, and Tilden. Third, for moral and technical support, I would like to thank my brothers Hoo, Paul and Long Ang of Brazil, Celso and Mariella Gálvez, Babu Parayil, and John and Christina Taran. Fourth, I would like to thank my husband, Donald R. Bissonnette, for all of the above reasons, and for taking care of our two sons, Alex and André Bissonnette, while I was working on the book and perfecting the recipes. Finally, I would like to thank all my cooking class students and friends for their encouragement to undertake this project. To all of the above, I offer my sincere thanks and gratitude.

Eng Tie Ang

Eng Tie Ang

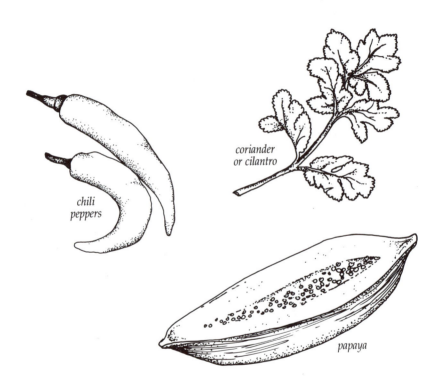

chili
peppers

coriander
or cilantro

papaya

Introduction

Brazil! What a country! What culture! What music! What dance! What beautiful people! What food! Yes, what food! From Bahia to Rio de Janeiro to Porto Alegre to Belém and everywhere in between, Brazil is a huge kitchen where women traditionally spent hours everyday in the planning and preparation of food. With the advent of modern appliances and conveniences, the time required to prepare these meals has been drastically reduced, yet the excellence of the food has remained constant. Brazilian cooking is easier to prepare, yet the same. How truly wonderful! It's a cuisine that has taken from a variety of cuisines and come up with a full and rich one of its own. Feijoada Completa, for example, is a dish whose origins can be traced to the Portuguese colonists, the African slaves and the indigenous people of Brazil. This wonderful synthesis of totally different cuisines is the national dish of Brazil.

Festas, Brazilian parties, are a big part of Brazilian culture, and almost any occasion is reason enough to have a festa in Brazil. And what is a festa without food. And what is a festa without delicious appetizers to sustain the family and guests while waiting for the main courses. And what kind of party is it if there is no tasty dessert to end the marvelous festa? And who makes all this wonderful food? Housewives and family cooks who take pride and joy in this work and in the presentation and enjoyment of their labors do. The pleasure and pride felt in a well-presented, delicious, and well-praised meal are genuinely valued rewards for the labor required to prepare a festa or any other meal.

The recipes in this book have been carefully selected for their genuine and unique authenticity and practicality in a modern kitchen. Most of them can be completed in an hour or so. Of course, like anything else, it's a matter of practice and familiarization: The more one does it, the easier it becomes. Try some of these recipes and prove me right. You'll be happy you did, and so will those fortunate enough to join you in your culinary delight.

Regarding supplies for Brazilian cooking, they are readily available in most places in the United States. Most supermarkets have all the supplies one needs for most of these recipes. Certainly, Latino markets carry whatever is needed. However, some supplies like manioc flour, dendê oil, and cachaça can only be found in larger cities or in certain areas of the country like the East Coast and southern California.

Delightful Brazilian Cooking is a compilation of recipes which I have gathered over the years and prepared for my family, friends, guests, and students. Some I have modified with consideration for health and well-being; consequently, egg count, sugar, salt, coconut milk, and oils have been kept to a minimum. However, all of these recipes are authentic in every other way. Also, special attention has been made to keep these recipes quick and easy- even for the novice cook. Finally, they are sure to bring delight to you and those lucky enough to share them with you.

About the Author

Eng Tie Ang was born in Indonesia to Chinese parents, moved to Brazil at the age of five, and came to the United States at the age of twenty-five. She learned cooking at an early age at home and in her parents' small restaurant in Suzano, São Paulo, Brazil. Her first and most influential cooking teacher was her mother, another great cook. She learned Brazilian cooking from her family cooks and from many Brazilian friends. As a teenager, she studied various kinds of cooking at a cooking school in her hometown. In addition to **Delightful Brazilian Cooking**, she has written and published **Delightful Thai Cooking**, a very highly praised collection of Thai recipes (also available from Ambrosia Publications). She is currently working on two other collections of recipes soon to be released: a tofu cookbook and an Indonesian cookbook.

In addition to writing cookbooks, Ms. Ang is a cooking instructor for the University of Washington's Experimental College in Seattle, Washington. She also frequently teaches courses through the Puget Consumers' Co-op. She has offered courses in Brazilian cooking, Thai cooking, Northern Italian cooking, Indonesian cooking, tofu cooking and vegetarian cooking. She also does catering for special events and is a food consultant. Moreover, she is an avid organic gardener and an accomplished batik painter.

Ms. Ang lives in Seattle with her husband, Donald R. Bissonnette, and two sons, Alex and André.

CHAPTER ONE

CONDIMENTS
&
SAUCES

garlic

ginger

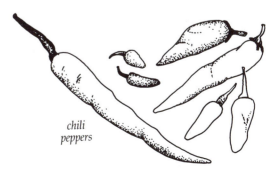

*chili
peppers*

Condiments and Sauces

Apple Sauce
(Molho de Maçã)

5 red apples, peeled, chopped
1 cup water
4 tablespoons sugar
1 tablespoon rum
2 tablespoons butter or
  margarine

In a small pot, cook the apples in the water until soft, then add the sugar and rum and simmer for 10 minutes. Add the butter and stir well. Serve hot or cold with poultry or pork.
Makes 4 cups.

Carrot Sauce
(Molho de Cenouras)

2 tablespoons butter or
  margarine
2 tablespoons white flour
1 cup chicken broth or milk
2 tablespoons ketchup
1 cup raw carrots, grated

Melt the butter in a small pot and brown the flour by putting it in the pot and stirring it with the butter for a couple of seconds. Gradually add the broth (or milk), ketchup and carrots and cook over low heat until the mixture thickens. Serve over meat. ***Makes 2 cups.***

Cucumber Pickle Sauce

(Molho de Pepino)

2 tablespoons butter or
  margarine
2 tablespoons white flour
1 cup dill pickle, finely
  chopped
1 cup milk
1 teaspoon ground white
  pepper

Melt the butter in a small pot and brown the flour by putting it in the pot and stirring it with the butter for a couple of seconds. Add the dill pickle, milk and pepper. Stir constantly over low heat for 3 minutes or until the mixture is creamy. Serve over meats. **Makes 2 cups.**

Curry Sauce

(Molho de Curry)

2 cups chicken broth
1/4 teaspoon salt
1 teaspoon ground white
  pepper
2 teaspoons ground curry
  powder
2 tablespoons rice flour,
  mixed with 2 tablespoons
  water

Bring the chicken broth to a boil in a small pot, then lower the heat. Add the salt, white pepper and curry powder. Gradually add rice flour, stirring until it becomes slightly thickened. Serve hot with any kind of fish. **Makes 2 cups.**

Dried Shrimp Sauce
(Molho de Acarajé)

5 dry malagueta peppers or 5
   fresh red hot cayenne
   peppers, finely minced
1/2 cup dried ground shrimp
   or 1/2 cup baby shrimp
1 medium onion, chopped
1/2 teaspoon salt
2 tablespoons dendê oil

In a blender, grind the peppers, shrimp, onion and salt into a paste. Heat the oil in a small frying pan and sauté the paste for about 5 minutes, stirring constantly. To be used as the filling for Deep-Fried Shrimp and Navy Beans (See page 92.).
Makes 1 cup.

Fish Sauce
(Molho para Peixe)

1 cup water
4 tablespoons white vinegar
1/4 teaspoon salt
1/2 teaspoon ground
   white pepper
3 egg yolks
2 tablespoons water
2 tablespoons butter or
   margarine, melted
1 tablespoon fresh lemon juice

In a small pot, bring the water with vinegar, salt and pepper to a boil until the mixture is reduced by half. Let cool. Mix egg yolks with the 2 tablespoons of water, butter and lemon juice and add to the cooled mixture. Put into a double boiler and cook until thick, stirring constantly. Keep warm in the double boiler until time to serve. Serve hot with any kind of fish. ***Makes 1 cup***.

Giblet Stuffing
(Farofa de Miudos)

2 tablespoons butter or
  margarine
1 small onion, chopped
3 cloves garlic, crushed
1 lb. chicken giblets, chopped
1/2 cup Italian parsley,
  chopped
1 teaspoon dried cayenne
  pepper flakes
2 cups manioc meal
1/2 teaspoon salt

Melt the butter in a large frying pan and sauté the onion and garlic until brown. Add the giblets, parsley and cayenne. Stir for 2 minutes. Add the manioc meal and salt and stir constantly until the mixture is loosely mixed. To be used for any kind of poultry stuffing. **Makes 2 cups.**

Manioc Meal with Butter and Egg
(Farofa com Manteiga e Ovos)

2 tablespoons butter or
  margarine
1 small yellow onion, finely
  chopped
2 eggs
2 cups manioc flour
2 tablespoons Italian
  parsley, finely chopped
1/2 teaspoon salt
1 teaspoon ground black
  pepper

Melt the butter in a large frying pan and sauté the onion until golden brown. Add the eggs and scramble until firm and separated in small pieces. Add the manioc meal, parsley, salt and pepper, stirring well until lightly browned. Serve with any bean dish. **Serves 6-8.**

Meat Sauce

(Molho de Carne)

2 tablespoons vegetable oil
  (See page 167.)
3 cloves garlic, crushed
1 medium onion, chopped
2 medium tomatoes, peeled,
  chopped
1/4 lb. lean ground beef
2 cups water
1/4 cup raisins
1/4 cup pitted green olives,
  chopped
2 tablespoons white wine
1/2 teaspoon salt
1 teaspoon ground white
  pepper

Heat the oil in a medium-sized pot and stir-fry the garlic and onion until golden brown. Add the tomatoes and ground beef. Simmer for 3 minutes and add the water, raisins, olives, wine, salt and pepper. Bring to a boil, then simmer for 25 minutes. Serve hot over Roast Leg of Pork (See page 112.). **Makes 2 cups.**

garlic

Pepper and Lemon Sauce
(Molho de Pimenta e Limão)

3 fresh red cayenne peppers,
   finely chopped
1 large yellow onion, finely
   chopped
2 cloves garlic, finely
   chopped
1/2 teaspoon salt
1/2 cup fresh lemon juice

In a small bowl, combine the pepper, onion, garlic, salt and lemon juice and stir until well-mixed. Refrigerate before serving. Serve over fish and meats. **Make 2 cups.**

Vinaigrette Sauce
(Molho Vinagrete)

1/2 cup olive oil
1 cup white vinegar
1 teaspoon salt
1 cup Italian parsley, finely
   chopped
4 large fresh tomatoes,
   chopped
1 large yellow onion, finely
   chopped
2 fresh red cayenne peppers,
   finely chopped (optional)

Combine all the ingredients in a large bowl. Stir well and serve either at room temperature or cold. Serve over meat and beans. **Make 3 cups.**

APPETIZERS

&

SNACKS

green
onions

shallots

CHAPTER TWO

Appetizers and Snacks

Baked Cheese Balls

(Bolinhos de Queijo)

1/2 cup margarine
1 cup white flour
1/2 cup Parmesan cheese
1 egg, beaten

In a small bowl, mix the margarine, flour and Parmesan cheese. Shape into small balls about 1 inch in diameter. Brush each one with the beaten egg. Place on a buttered baking sheet and bake in a 375 degree oven for 15 minutes or until the top is golden. **Makes 12 balls.**

Beef Kabobs with Onion and Pepper

(Espetinhos de Carne de Vaca com Cebola e Pimentão)

1 lb. tenderloin beef, cut into
  1/2 inch cubes
1 large red bell pepper, cut
  into 1 inch cubes
1 large green bell pepper, cut
  into 1 inch cubes
1 large yellow onion, cut into
  1 inch cubes
1 teaspoon ground black
  pepper
1 teaspoon salt
juice of 1 lemon
3 cloves garlic, crushed
3 bay leaves, crushed
1/4 cup olive oil
6" bamboo skewers, soaked
  in water for 15 minutes

Place the beef, red pepper, green pepper and onion in a large bowl. Set aside. In a small bowl, mix together the pepper, salt, lemon, garlic, bay leaves and oil. Pour this mixture over the cubed beef and vegetables and marinate for at least 1 hour or overnight, refrigerated. Alternate vegetables and beef cubes on bamboo skewers. Broil over a hot charcoal fire until cooked thoroughly, or broil in the oven for 3 minutes on each side.

Makes 24 skewers.

Chicken Balls

(Coxinha de Frango)

4 cups water
2 whole boneless chicken
  breasts, skinned
2 tablespoons olive oil
4 cloves garlic, crushed
1 small onion, finely chopped
1/2 cup Italian parsley,
  chopped
2 small tomatoes, peeled,
  seeded, chopped
1 teaspoon salt
1 teaspoon ground white
  pepper
4 cups milk
4 cups whites flour, sifted
1/2 cup fine corn meal
1 teaspoon sugar
1/2 cup margarine
2 cups vegetable oil for deep-
  frying (See page 167.)

In a deep pot, bring the water to a boil. Add the chicken and simmer for 30 minutes. Remove the chicken and cut into small cubes. Reserve the chicken broth. Heat the oil in a frying pan and sauté the garlic and onion until golden. Add the chicken cubes, parsley, tomatoes, salt and pepper. Stir-fry for 3 minutes. Set aside. In the large deep pot with the broth from the chicken add the milk, flour, corn meal, sugar and margarine. Stir well and cook over low heat, stirring constantly until the mixture pulls away from the sides of the pan. Let cool. Put a little oil on each of your palms and make small balls about 2 inches in diameter with a small cavity about 1 inch deep in each. Fill with 1 teaspoon of the chicken mixture. Close the hole and shape again into a small ball. Deep-fry in hot oil until golden brown on both sides. Remove and drain on paper towels.

Makes 30 chicken balls.

Chicken Squares

(Salgado Americano)

3 eggs
1 1/2 cups milk
1 cup vegetable oil (See
  page 167.)
1 teaspoon salt
1 1/2 cups white flour
1 tablespoon baking powder
1 teaspoon ground white
  pepper
2 cups cooked chicken breast,
  skinned, cubed
2 hard-boiled eggs, sliced
1 small onion, thinly sliced
1 small red tomato, sliced
1/4 cup stuffed green olives,
  sliced
4 tablespoons grated
  Parmesan cheese

In a blender, blend the eggs, milk, oil, salt, flour, baking powder and pepper until thoroughly mixed. Pour into a buttered 9x13 inch baking pan. Layer the chicken, sliced eggs, onion, tomato, green olives and the Parmesan cheese on top. Bake in a 375 degree oven for 30 minutes or until the top is browned. Cool. Cut into small squares.
Serves 4-6.

Cod Fish Croquettes

(Bolinhos de Bacalhau)

1 lb. dried cod fish

1 quart water

3 tablespoons margarine

2 tablespoons Italian parsley, chopped

1 large potato, peeled, boiled, pureed

1 cup white flour

1 cup milk

3 eggs, separated

2 cups vegetable oil for deep-frying (See page 167.)

*In a bowl, soak the cod fish in water overnight. Then drain and remove the skin and bones. In a small pot, bring the quart of water to a boil, add the cod fish and boil for 3 minutes. Discard the water. Shred the cod fish. In a large pot, add the shredded cod fish, margarine, parsley, potato, flour, milk and yolks. Stir well and cook over low heat, stirring constantly until the mixture pulls away from the sides of the pan. Let cool. Put a little oil on each of your palms and make small cro-quettes (oval shaped) about 2 inches long. Coat each croquette with beaten egg whites on both sides and deep-fry in hot oil until golden brown. Remove and drain on paper towels. **Makes 12.***

Deep-Fried Bulghar Wheat with Ground Beef and Herbs
(Kibe)

1 cup dry bulghar wheat,
  soaked overnight in water
1 lb. lean ground beef
4 cloves garlic, crushed
1 teaspoon salt
1/2 cup Italian parsley, finely
  chopped
2 tablespoons fresh mint, minced
1 teaspoon ground black pepper
2 cups vegetable oil for
  deep-frying (See page 167.)
2 lemons, cut into wedges

In a large bowl, add the drained bulghar wheat, beef, garlic, salt, parsley, mint and pepper and mix thoroughly. Form into 2 inch ovals. Deep fry in hot oil until golden. Remove and drain on paper towels. Garnish with lemon wedges. ***Makes 24 kibes.***

mint

Delicious Cheese Ball Appetizers
(Salgadinhos Deliciosos)

2 tablespoons Italian parsley, finely chopped
1/4 cup sour cream
1/2 cup chopped ham
1/4 cup chopped green olives
1 tablespoon chopped dill pickle
1 cup grated Parmesan cheese
1 cup chopped roasted penuts
2 tablespoons Dijon mustard
24 crackers

In a large bowl, mix the parsley, sour cream, ham, olives, chopped dill pickle and Parmesan cheese. Make small balls 1/2 inch in diameter and coat each with chopped peanuts. Spread mustard on each cracker and place a cheese ball on each.
Makes 24 canapés.

Delightful Cheese Bread
(Delicias de Queijo)

 8 tablespoons cream cheese
10 tablespoons grated Parmesan cheese
1 tablespoon butter or margarine
2 egg yolks, beaten
1/2 teaspoon nutmeg
12 slices rye bread, lightly toasted

In a small bowl, combine the cream cheese, Parmesan cheese, butter, egg yolks and nutmeg. Cut each slice of bread in half and remove crust. Spread the cheese mixture on each slice of bread. Put on a buttered baking sheet and bake in a 350 degree oven for 10 minutes. Serve hot. ***Makes 24 canapés.***

Ground Beef Croquettes

(Bolinhos de Carne)

2 tablespoons olive oil
4 cloves garlic, crushed
1 small onion, finely chopped
2 lbs. lean ground beef
1/4 cup Italian parsley, finely
  chopped
1 teaspoon salt
1 teaspoon ground black
  pepper
2 cups white bread, cubed,
  without crusts
1/2 cup milk
3 eggs, separated
2 cups bread crumbs
2 cups vegetable oil for deep-
  frying (See page 167.)

Heat the oil in a deep pot and sauté the garlic and onion until golden brown. Add the ground beef, parsley, salt and pepper and stir for 5 minutes. Set aside. Soak the bread in the milk and add to the ground beef mixture along with the 3 egg yolks. Mix well and cook over a low flame, stirring constantly until the mixture pulls away from the sides of the pan. Let cool, then make small balls about 2 inches in diameter. Coat each one with beaten egg whites on both sides and roll in bread crumbs. Deep-fry in hot oil until golden brown. Remove and drain on paper towels. **Makes 24 croquettes.**

Ham Patties

(Bolinhos de Presunto)

2 cups milk
2 cups white flour
1 cup finely chopped ham
3 tablespoons margarine,
   melted
1 teaspoon salt
1 teaspoon ground white
   pepper
1/4 teaspoon nutmeg
3 eggs, separated
2 cups vegetable oil for deep-
   frying (See page 167.)

In a large pot, mix the milk with flour until it forms a smooth paste. Add the ham, margarine, salt, pepper, nutmeg and yolks. Put over a low flame and cook, stirring constantly, until the mixture pulls away from the sides of the pot. Cool. Make small patties about 2 inches in diameter. Coat each pattie with beaten egg whites on both sides and deep-fry in hot oil until golden brown. Remove and drain on paper towels. Serve hot. **Makes 24 patties.**

Shrimp and Palm Heart Turnovers

(Empadas de Camarão com Palmito)

2 1/2 cups white flour, sifted
1/2 teaspoon salt
1/2 cup butter or margarine
4 egg yolks
2 tablespoons vegetable oil
  (See page 167.)
1 small onion, finely chopped
2 cloves garlic, minced
1 cup cooked baby shrimp
1 cup palm hearts, finely
  chopped
2 tablespoons white flour
4 tablespoons milk
1/2 teaspoon salt
muffin tins

*Make the dough in a large bowl by thoroughly mixing the 2 1/2 cups of flour, salt, butter and 2 of the egg yolks. Set aside. Heat the oil in a large frying pan and sauté the onion and garlic until golden brown. Add the shrimp and palm hearts and stir for 2 minutes. Add the 2 tablespoons of flour, milk and salt and stir constantly until the mixture is creamy. Let cool. Roll out the dough into circles 3 inches in diameter and place into individually buttered muffin tins. Fill with a tablespoon of the shrimp and palm heart mixture and cover with another piece of dough 3 inches in diameter. Seal the edge and brush each one with the remaining 2 beaten egg yolks. Bake in a 375 degree oven for 20 minutes or until the top of the dough is light golden brown. Cool. Remove from muffin tins and place in small paper baking cups. **Makes 24 turnovers.***

Shrimp Balls

(Bolinhos de Camarão)

2 tablespoons olive oil
1 lb. medium shrimp, shelled,
  deveined, chopped
  (See diagram, page 163.)
1 yellow onion, finely chopped
1 teaspoon ground cumin
1 teaspoon ground coriander
1 teaspoon salt
1 teaspoon ground white
  pepper
2 tablespoons Italian parsley,
  chopped
1 cup white flour
1 cup milk
3 eggs, beaten
2 cups bread crumbs
2 cups vegetable oil for
  deep-frying (See page 167.)

Heat the olive oil in a large frying pan and sauté the shrimp with onion, cumin, coriander, salt, pepper and parsley for 3 minutes. In a large pot, place the flour, milk and the shrimp mixture and mix well. Bring to a boil. Then cook over a low flame, stirring constantly, until the mixture pulls away from the sides of the pot. Let cool and make small balls about 2 inches in diameter. Coat each ball with beaten eggs on both sides and roll in bread crumbs. Deep-fry in hot oil until golden brown. Remove and drain on paper towels. **Makes 24 balls.**

Shrimp Kabobs with Garlic

(Espetinhos de Camarão com Alho)

4 tablespoons olive oil
4 cloves garlic, crushed
4 tablespoons Italian parsley,
  chopped
1 teaspoon salt
1 teaspoon ground white
  pepper
juice of 1 lemon
2 large onions, cut into 1 inch
  cubes
2 lbs. large shrimp, shelled,
  deveined (See diagram,
  page 163.)
6" bamboo skewers,
  soaked in water for 15
  minutes

In a large bowl, mix the oil, garlic, parsley, salt, pepper, lemon juice and onion. Add the shrimp and marinate for at least 1 hour or overnight, refrigerated. Alternate the onion and shrimp on bamboo skewers. Broil over a hot charcoal fire until cooked, or broil in the oven for 3 minutes on each side. **Makes 20 skewers.**

Tapioca Bread with Cheese
(Pão de Queijo)

2/3 cup vegetable oil
  (See page 167.)
2 cups milk
4 cups tapioca flour
2 eggs, beaten
1 1/2 cups grated Parmesan
  cheese

Combine the oil and milk in a pan and bring to a boil. Put the tapioca flour in a bowl, add the boiling mixture and mix well with a wooden spoon. Add the beaten eggs and mix well. Add the Parmesan cheese and mix well again. Let the mixture stand for 10 minutes. Put a little oil on each of your palms and make small balls, 2 inches in diameter. (Make sure when forming the balls that your hands are always lightly oiled.) Place on a buttered baking sheet and bake in a 350 degree oven for about 20 minutes or until the top is light brown. **Makes 30 small cheese breads.**

CHAPTER THREE

SOUPS

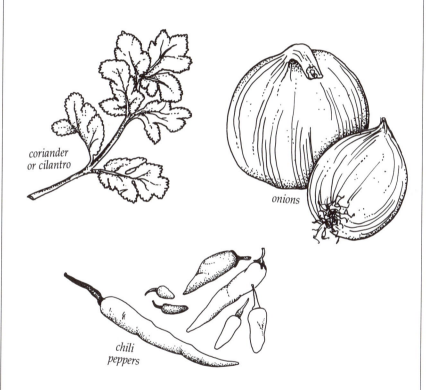

coriander
or cilantro

onions

chili
peppers

Soups

Artichoke Heart Soup

(Sopa de Alcachofras)

6 cups water
12 artichoke hearts, chopped
1 onion, chopped
1 teaspoon salt
2 cups milk
6 tablespoons fine corn meal
2 tablespoons butter or
  margarine
8 tablespoons grated
  Parmesan cheese
2 tablespoons Italian parsley,
  chopped
1/2 cup croutons

Put the water in a medium-sized pot. Add the chopped artichoke hearts, onion and salt and simmer for about 30 minutes or until the artichoke is soft. Mix the milk with corn meal and add to the soup. Cook until it thickens. Add the butter, cheese and parsley. Garnish with croutons.
Serves 6-8.

Beef Stock for Soup

(Caldo de Carne)

4 quarts water
2 lbs. round steak, sliced
1 teaspoon salt
2 yellow onions, chopped
6 cloves garlic, crushed
6 carrots, sliced
1/4 cup fresh leeks, chopped
1/4 cup Italian parsley,
  chopped
1 bay leaf

Boil the meat in a large pot. As it boils, skim off the fat, then add the salt, onions, garlic, carrots, leeks, Italian parsley and bay leaf. Cover and simmer for about 2 hours or until meat is tender. Cool and strain. Discard the vegetables and use the beef and stock for soup or consommé.
Makes 3 quarts.

Black Bean Soup

(Sopa de Feijão Preto)

1 tablespoon vegetable oil
  (See page 167.)
4 strips bacon, finely chopped
3 cups cooked black beans,
  mashed
5 cups beef stock
  (See page 37.)
1 yellow onion, chopped
2 bay leaves
2 large tomatoes, peeled,
  chopped
1/4 teaspoon salt
1 hard boiled egg, sliced
1/2 cup croutons

Heat the oil in a medium-sized pot and stir-fry the bacon until golden brown. Add the mashed black beans, beef stock, onion, bay leaves, tomatoes and salt. Simmer for 30 minutes, stirring occasionally. Garnish with sliced egg and croutons.
Serves 6-8.

onions

Brazilian Stewed Chicken

(Ensopado de Galinha com Legumes)

2 tablespoons olive oil
3 cloves garlic, crushed
1 small yellow onion, chopped
2 lbs. drumsticks
2 lbs. boneless chicken breasts,
  cut into 1 inch cubes
1 teaspoon salt
2 tablespoons Italian parsley,
  chopped
4 large tomatoes, peeled,
  chopped
1 teaspoon ground white
  pepper
3 large potatoes, peeled, cut
  into 2 inch cubes
3 large carrots, sliced
1 cup celery, chopped
4 cups water

Heat the oil in a medium-sized pot and sauté the garlic and onion until golden brown. Add the drumsticks and cubed chicken breasts. Stir-fry for 3 minutes. Add the salt, Italian parsley, tomatoes, pepper, potatoes, carrots, celery and water. Cook over low heat for about 30 minutes or until the chicken and vegetables are tender. **Serves 6-8.**

Carrot Soup

(Sopa de Cenouras)

2 tablespoons butter or
  margarine
1 yellow onion, finely chopped
3 cloves garlic, crushed
4 cups raw carrots, chopped
1 teaspoon ground white
  pepper
1/2 teaspoon salt
4 cups water
2 tablespoons Italian parsley
1/2 cup grated Parmesan
  cheese

Melt the butter in a medium-sized pot and stir-fry the onion and garlic until light brown. Add the carrots, pepper, salt and water and simmer for about 30 minutes or until carrots are completely soft. Let cool and use a blender or a food processor to purée the carrot mixture. Garnish with Italian parsley and Parmesan cheese. **Serves 6.**

Chicken Soup

(Canja de Galinha)

3-4 lb. chicken, cut into small pieces
3 quarts water
1 teaspoon salt
1 teaspoon ground white pepper
1 cup white long grain rice, washed, drained
1 yellow onion, chopped
1 carrot, finely diced
1 clove garlic, crushed
3 medium tomatoes, peeled, seeded, chopped
1 tablespoon fresh Italian parsley, finely chopped
1 tablespoon green onion, chopped

In a large pot, combine the chicken, water, salt and white pepper and cook for 1 hour or until the chicken is tender. Add the rice, onion, carrot, garlic and tomatoes and simmer until rice is well-cooked, approximately 30 minutes. Garnish with parsley and green onion. ***Serves 6-8.***

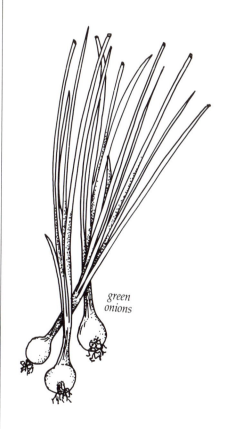

green onions

Lentil Soup

(Sopa de Lentilhas)

2 cups lentils, washed, soaked
  overnight, drained
5 cups water
2 tablespoons butter or
  margarine
1 cup yellow onion, finely
  chopped
3 cloves garlic, crushed
1 teaspoon salt
1 teaspoon ground black
  pepper
2 cups beef stock or water
  (See page 37.)
4 tablespoons Parmesan
  cheese

*In a medium-sized pot,
cook the lentils in water over
medium heat about 1 hour or until
the lentils are done. Purée the
lentils in a blender and return to
pot. Melt the butter in a frying pan
and sauté the onion and garlic
until light golden brown. Add the
sautéed onions, salt, pepper and
beef stock to the lentils. Let simmer
for 10 minutes. Garnish with
Parmesan cheese.*
Serves 6-8.

Manioc Soup

(Sopa de Mandioca)

2 tablespoons butter or
  margarine
1 lb. manioc root, peeled,
  chopped
1 yellow onion, chopped
4 large tomatoes, peeled,
  seeded
1/2 cup celery, chopped
1/2 cup carrots, chopped
1 quart water or beef stock
  (See page 37.)
1/4 teaspoon salt
1 teaspoon ground black
  pepper
2 tablespoons Italian parsley,
  chopped

Melt the butter in a medium-sized pot and sauté the manioc root and onion for 2 minutes. Add the tomatoes, celery, carrots, water, salt and pepper. Cook over low heat for about 30 minutes or until the manioc is soft. Garnish with Italian parsley. **Serves 4-6.**

Mixed Vegetable Soup

(Sopa de Legumes)

2 tablespoons butter or
  margarine
1 yellow onion, finely chopped
4 cloves garlic, crushed
2 medium potatoes, cubed
3 carrots, cubed
2 stalks celery, diced
2 small sweet potatoes, diced
2 medium zucchini, diced
3 fresh tomatoes, peeled,
  seeded, chopped
1 leek, finely chopped
1 quart water or beef stock
  (See page 37.)
1/4 teaspoon salt

Melt the butter in a medium-sized pot and stir-fry the onion and garlic until light brown. Add the potatoes, carrots, celery, sweet potatoes, zucchini, tomatoes, leek, water and salt. Simmer for about 30 minutes or until the vegetables are soft.
Serves 4-6.

Onion Soup

(Sopa de Cebola)

2 tablespoons butter or
  margarine
4 medium yellow onions,
  thinly sliced
2 tablespoons white flour
2 quarts beef stock
  (See page 37.)
1 teaspoon ground white
  pepper
8 slices toasted French bread,
  buttered on both sides
1 cup grated Parmesan cheese

Melt the butter in a medium-sized pot and sauté the onions until light brown. Add the flour to the onions and mix thoroughly. Then add the stock and pepper to the onions and cook for 20 minutes. Fill 8 individual oven-proof bowls with soup. On top of each bowl, put one slice of toast and sprinkle with Parmesan cheese. Bake for about 10 minutes in a preheated oven at 400 degrees. **Serves 8.**

onions

Pumpkin Soup

(Sopa de Abóbora)

2 tablespoons butter or
  margarine
1 yellow onion, finely chopped
4 cloves garlic, crushed
2 lbs. pumpkin, peeled,
  seeded, cubed
1 teaspoon salt
1 teaspoon ground black
  pepper
4 cups water
4 tablespoons grated
  Parmesan cheese
2 tablespoons Italian parsley,
  chopped

Melt the butter in a medium-sized pot and stir-fry the onion and garlic until light brown. Add the pumpkin, salt, pepper and water and simmer for about 30 minutes or until the pumpkin is completely soft. Let cool. Purée the pumpkin in a blender or food processor. Garnish with Parmesan cheese and Italian parsley. Serve hot or cold.
Serves 6-8.

Seafood Soup

(Sopa de Frutos do Mar)

2 tablespoons olive oil

1 small onion, finely chopped

3 cloves garlic, crushed

1 lb. sea bass, cut into 1-inch
squares

4 large fresh tomatoes, peeled,
seeded

1 teaspoon ground coriander

1 teaspoon salt

2 quarts water

1 can dungeness crab meat
(6 oz.)

2 cans minced clams
(7 oz. each)

1 cup cooked lobster meat

1 cup cooked baby shrimp

1 fresh red cayenne pepper,
chopped

4 tablespoons green onion,
chopped

2 tablespoons Italian parsley,
chopped

*Heat the oil in a large pot
and stir-fry the onion and garlic
until golden brown. Add the fish
and tomatoes and sauté for 2
minutes. Add the coriander, salt
and water and bring to a boil. Add
the crab meat, clams, lobster,
shrimp and cayenne. Simmer for
3 minutes. Garnish with green
onion and Italian parsley.*
Serves 6-8.

Shrimp with Cream of Corn Soup

(Sopa de Milho com Camarão)

2 tablespoons vegetable oil
(See page 167.)
1 yellow onion, finely
chopped
3 cloves garlic, crushed
2 quarts water
2 cans creamed corn
(17 oz. each)
1 teaspoon salt
1 teaspoon ground black
pepper
1 lb. baby shrimp, cooked
2 tablespoons cornstarch,
dissolved in 4 tablespoons
of cold water

Heat the oil in a large pot and stir-fry the onion and garlic until light golden brown. Add the water and cream of corn. Bring to a boil and reduce the temperature to low. Add the salt, black pepper, shrimp and cornstarch mixture. Stir well and simmer for 3 minutes.
Serves 6-8.

Sweet Potato Soup

(Sopa de Batata Doce)

2 tablespoons butter or
  margarine
1 small yellow onion, finely
  chopped
3 cloves garlic, crushed
6 tablespoons Italian parsley,
  finely chopped
4 fresh tomatoes, peeled,
  seeded
1 lb. sweet potatoes, cooked,
  mashed
1 cup milk
1 quart water or beef stock
  (See page 37.)
1/4 teaspoon salt
1 teaspoon ground white
  pepper
2 tablespoons green onion,
  chopped

Melt the butter in a large pot and sauté the onion, garlic and Italian parsley for 3 minutes. Add the tomatoes, sweet potatoes, milk, water, salt and pepper. Bring to a boil, stirring constantly until the soup thickens. Garnish with green onions. **Serves 6.**

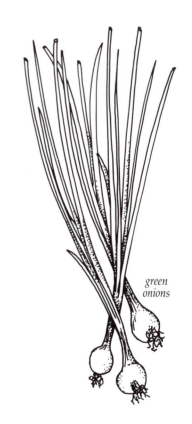

green onions

49

Watercress Soup with Corn

(Sopa de Agrião com Milho)

2 tablespoons vegetable oil
  (See page 167.)
1 yellow onion, chopped
3 cloves garlic, crushed
2 quarts water or beef stock
  (See page 37.)
1 can creamed corn (17 oz.)
1 can whole corn (17 oz.),
  drained
1/4 teaspoon salt
1 teaspoon ground white
  pepper
1 bunch watercress, washed,
  chopped

Heat the oil in a large pot and stir-fry the onion and garlic until light golden brown. Add the water, creamed corn, whole corn, salt and pepper. Bring to a boil for 5 minutes. Reduce the temperature to low and add the watercress. Simmer for 1 minute. **Serves 6-8.**

CHAPTER FOUR

SALADS

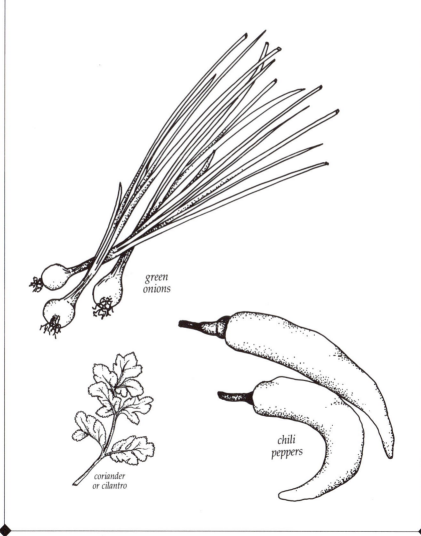

green
onions

coriander
or cilantro

chili
peppers

Salads

Beet Salad
(Salada de Beterraba)

4 beets, boiled, thinly sliced
1 yellow onion, thinly sliced
3 cloves garlic, crushed
1/2 teaspoon salt
1 teaspoon dried oregano
juice of 1 lime
1/4 cup olive oil

Arrange the beets with the onion on a large platter. In a small bowl, mix the garlic, salt, oregano, lime and olive oil. Pour the dressing over the salad. Refrigerate before serving.
Serves 4-6.

Broccoli Salad
(Salada de Brócolis)

2 lbs. fresh broccoli, cut into
   small florets
2 large potatoes, boiled, cubed
3 tomatoes, sliced
4 tablespoons chopped green
   onion
1/4 teaspoon salt
1/2 teaspoon ground
   black pepper
1/2 cup mayonnaise
juice of 1 lime
1/4 cup olive oil
2 hard boiled eggs, sliced
   (optional)

Cook the broccoli in a steamer for 3 minutes or until just tender and bright green. Remove from the heat and rinse under cold water. Drain. Place the broccoli with potatoes on a bed of tomatoes on a large platter and refrigerate. In a small bowl, mix the green onion, salt, pepper, mayonnaise, lime and oil. Pour the dressing over the salad just before serving. Garnish with sliced eggs. ***Serves 4-6.***

Broiled Bell Pepper Salad
(Salada de Pimentão)

4 green bell peppers
4 red bell peppers
1 yellow onion, thinly sliced
1/2 teaspoon salt
6 tablespoons red vinegar
1/4 cup olive oil

Broil the peppers in a large baking pan for 2-3 minutes on each side. Remove the skins and seeds by placing the peppers in a plastic bag and allowing them to cool. (This allows skins to be removed more easily.) Slice the peppers and place them in a bowl with the onion, salt, vinegar and olive oil. Mix well. **Serves 4-6.**

Cauliflower Salad
(Salada de Couve Flor)

2 lbs. cauliflower, boiled, cut into small florets
1 small yellow onion, thinly sliced
1 bunch watercress, washed, drained
4 tablespoons Italian parsley, chopped
1/2 teaspoon salt
1 teaspoon ground black pepper
juice of 1 lime
1/4 cup olive oil

Cook the cauliflower by adding florets to a large pot of boiling water and simmering until just tender. Drain and plunge the florets into very cold water. Place the cauliflower and onion on a bed of watercress on a large platter and refrigerate the vegetables before serving. In a small bowl, mix the parsley, salt, pepper, lime and olive oil. Pour the dressing over the salad just before serving. **Serves 4-6.**

Chayote Squash Salad

(Salada de Chuchu)

1 quart water
6 chayote squash, peeled,
  cores removed
3 cloves garlic, crushed
1 large onion, thinly sliced
1/2 teaspoon salt
1/2 teaspoon ground
  black pepper
6 tablespoons Italian parsley,
  chopped
1/4 cup olive oil
5 tablespoons white vinegar

Bring the water to a boil in a deep pot. Put the chayote squash into the boiling water and boil for 10 minutes; do not overcook. Drain in a colander. Slice the squash and place in a salad bowl with garlic, onion, salt, pepper, parsley, oil and vinegar. Mix well and refrigerate before serving. ***Serves 4-6.***

Chicken Salad

(Salada de Frango)

2 cups cooked chicken,
  skinned, diced
1 cup boiled string beans,
  diced
2 large boiled potatoes, diced
2 large boiled carrots, diced
2 hard boiled eggs, diced
1/2 teaspoon ground black
  pepper
2 teaspoons mustard
1 cup mayonnaise
3 large tomatoes, sliced
1/2 cup stuffed green olives

*In a large bowl, mix well the chicken, beans, potatoes, carrots, eggs, pepper, mustard and mayonnaise. Place the salad on the bed of tomatoes. Garnish with olives. Refrigerate before serving. **Serves 4-6.***

Cucumber Salad

(Salada de Pepino)

2 large cucumbers, peeled,
  sliced
1 large yellow onion, thinly
  sliced
4 tablespoons Italian parsley,
  chopped
1/2 teaspoon salt
1/2 teaspoon ground
  black pepper
4 tablespoons white vinegar
5 tablespoons olive oil

*Arrange the cucumbers, onion and parsley in layers on a large serving platter. In a bowl, mix the salt, pepper, vinegar and oil. Pour the dressing over the cucumbers. Refrigerate before serving. **Serves 4-6.***

Eggplant Salad

(Salada de Beringela)

2 large eggplants
2 large tomatoes, chopped
3 cloves garlic, crushed
1 large onion, chopped
1/2 cup Italian parsley,
  chopped
1 teaspoon salt
juice of 1 lime
1/2 cup olive oil

*Bring water to a boil in a large pot. Add the whole eggplants and cook for 20 minutes; do not overcook. Drain. Cut the eggplants into 2 inch squares, leaving the peel on. Combine the eggplant, tomatoes, garlic, onion, parsley, salt, lime juice and olive oil in a large salad bowl. Mix well and refrigerate. **Servers 4-6.***

Garbanzo Bean Salad

(Salada de Grão de Bico)

2 cans garbanzo beans (20 oz. each), drained
1 small onion, chopped
2 tablespoons Italian parsley, chopped
2 large tomatoes, chopped
1/2 teaspoon salt
1/2 teaspoon ground black pepper
1/4 cup olive oil

Combine the garbanzo beans, onion, parsley, tomatoes, salt, pepper and olive oil in a large salad bowl. Mix well and refrigerate. **Serves 4-6.**

Green Cabbage Salad

(Salada de Repolho)

1 small green cabbage, thinly sliced
4 tablespoons Italian parsley, chopped
1/2 teaspoon salt
1 teaspoon ground white pepper
juice of 2 limes
1/2 cup olive oil

Combine the cabbage, parsley, salt, pepper, lime juice and olive oil in a large salad bowl. Mix well and refrigerate before serving. **Serves 4-6.**

Green Leaf Lettuce Salad with Tomatoes

(Salada de Alface com Tomates)

1 head of green leaf lettuce, washed, spun dry
4 large tomatoes, sliced
1 small yellow onion, sliced
1/2 teaspoon salt
4 tablespoons white vinegar
1/4 cup olive oil

Place the lettuce leaves on a large serving platter and arrange the tomatoes and onion in layers. Refrigerate before serving. In a small bowl, mix the salt, vinegar and oil. Pour the dressing over the salad just before serving. **Serves 4-6.**

Palm Heart Salad

(Salada de Palmito)

1 can palm hearts (20 oz.), drained, sliced
2 large tomatoes, sliced
1 cucumber, peeled, sliced
1 small yellow onion, sliced
1/2 cup stuffed green olives
1/2 teaspoon salt
juice of 1 lime
1/4 cup olive oil
2 hard boiled eggs, sliced

Place the palm heart slices on a large serving platter and arrange the tomatoes, cucumber, onion and olives in layers. Refrigerate before serving. In a small bowl, mix the salt, lime juice and oil. Pour the dressing over the salad and garnish with eggs just before serving. **Serves 4-6.**

Shrimp Salad with Artichoke

(Salada de Camarão com Alcachofras)

1 cup cooked artichoke hearts
2 cups cooked baby shrimp
1 cup carrots, grated
1 teaspoon Worcestershire
   sauce
1 teaspoon ground white
   pepper
1 cup mayonnaise
1 bunch watercress, washed,
   drained

Thoroughly mix the artichoke hearts, shrimp, carrots, Worcestershire, pepper and mayonnaise in a large bowl. Place the salad on a bed of watercress. Refrigerate before serving.
Serves 4-6.

Watercress Salad

(Salada de Agrião)

2 bunches watercress, washed,
   drained
1 yellow onion, thinly sliced
1/2 teaspoon salt
juice of 1 lime
1/4 cup olive oil

Arrange the watercress with the onion on a large platter. In a small bowl, mix the salt, lime juice and oil. Before serving, pour the dressing over the salad.
Serves 4.

CHAPTER FIVE

VEGETABLES

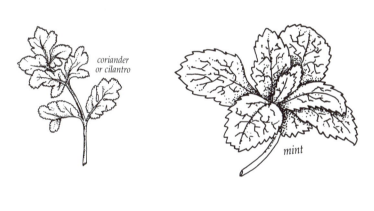

coriander or cilantro

mint

chili peppers

CHAPTER FIVE

Vegetables

Cauliflower with Cheese

(Couve Flor com Queijo)

1 quart water
2 lbs. fresh cauliflower, washed, cut into small florets
2 tablespoons butter or margarine
3 tablespoons white flour
1/2 teaspoon nutmeg
2 cups milk
2 egg yolks, beaten
1/2 cup grated Parmesan cheese
4 tablespoons Italian parsley, chopped

Bring the water to a boil in a deep pot. Put the cauliflower into the boiling water for 3 minutes; do not overcook. Drain in a colander. In a large frying pan, brown the butter and flour by stirring them for a couple of seconds over low heat. Add the nutmeg, milk and yolk. Cook until it thickens. Place the cauliflower in a 9x13 inch baking dish, cover with the sauce, cheese and Italian parsley. Bake the cauliflower at 350 degrees for 20 minutes or until the cheese becomes brown on top. **Serves 4-6.**

Chayote Squash Fritters

(Bolinhos de Chuchu)

1 quart water
4 chayote squash, peeled,
   cores removed, cut in half
1 small yellow onion, chopped
3 cloves garlic, minced
1 teaspoon salt
1 teaspoon ground white
   pepper
4 tablespoons Italian parsley,
   finely chopped
1 egg, beaten
1 cup white flour
2 cups vegetable oil for deep-
   frying (See page 167.)

Bring the water to a boil in a deep pot. Add the squash and cook for 10 minutes or until the squash is tender. Drain and mash the squash. In a bowl, mix the squash, onion, garlic, salt, pepper, parsley, egg and flour. Heat the oil in a frying pan over medium-high heat for 1 minute. Carefully drop in a tablespoon of the squash mixture for each fritter. Fry until golden brown on both sides. Remove and drain on paper towels. **Serves 4-6.**

Chayote Squash Soufflé

(Soufflé de Chuchu)

1 quart water
4 chayote squash, peeled, cores removed
1 tablespoon butter or margarine
2 tablespoons flour
1/2 cup milk
1/2 teaspoon salt
1 teaspoon ground white pepper
2 eggs, separated
4 tablespoons Parmesan cheese

*Bring the water to a boil in a deep pot. Put the chayote squash into boiling water and boil for 10 minutes or until soft. Drain and mash the squash. Melt the butter in a large frying pan and sauté the flour until light brown. Add the milk, salt, pepper, beaten egg yolks and mashed squash. Mix well and fold in stiffly-beaten egg whites. Pour into a buttered 9x13 inch baking pan and sprinkle with Parmesan cheese. Bake at 375 degrees in a preheated oven for about 20 minutes or until brown. **Serves 4-6.***

Collard Greens

(Couve Refogada)

2 tablespoons vegetable oil
(See page 167.)
3 cloves garlic, crushed
2 bunches collard greens,
washed, shredded
1 teaspoon salt

Heat the oil in a large frying pan and sauté the garlic until light golden brown. Add the collard greens and salt. Stir-fry over medium-high heat for 3 minutes or until greens are tender; do not overcook. Serve with Brazilian Black Bean.(See page 127.). **Serves 4-6.**

garlic

Corn Fritters

(Bolinhos de Milho)

4 ears corn, shucked
1 small yellow onion, chopped
3 cloves garlic, crushed
1 egg, beaten
1 teaspoon salt
1 teaspoon ground white
   pepper
1 cup white flour
1 1/2 cups vegetable oil for
   deep-frying (See page 167.)

Blend the shucked corn with the onion, garlic and egg in a blender until finely minced. Pour the mixture in a large bowl with salt, pepper and flour and thoroughly mix. Heat the oil over medium-high heat in a large frying pan and drop in a tablespoon of the mixture for each fritter. Fry until light brown on both sides. Remove and drain on paper towels. **Serves 4-6.**

Corn Meal Mush

(Polenta de Milho)

1 cup fine yellow cornmeal
1 cup cold water
1/2 teaspoon salt
2 cups boiling water
2 tablespoons butter or
  margarine
1/2 cup tomato sauce
3/4 cup grated Parmesan
  cheese

*In a medium-sized pot, combine the cornmeal, cold water and salt. Add the boiling water and butter and stir constantly over low heat for about 15 minutes or until the mixture is thick enough to hold its shape. Pour into a buttered 9 inch round baking dish. Let cool. Turn the baking dish upside down on a platter and unmold the mush. Serve with tomato sauce. Sprinkle with Parmesan cheese. **Serves 4-6.***

Palm Heart with Onion and Tomatoes

(Palmito com Cebola e Tomates)

2 tablespoons butter or
  margarine
3 cloves garlic, crushed
1 large yellow onion, thinly
  sliced
2 large tomatoes, chopped
1 cup palm heart, sliced
1/2 teaspoon salt
1 teaspoon ground black
  pepper
4 tablespoons Italian parsley,
  chopped
2 tablespoons fresh lime juice

Melt the butter in a large frying pan and sauté the garlic and onion until light brown. Add the tomatoes, palm heart, salt and pepper. Stir-fry for 3 minutes. Garnish with Italian parsley and lime juice. **Serves 4-6.**

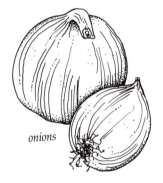

onions

Pumpkin Soufflé

(Soufflé de Abóbora)

3 cups pumpkin, pureed
1/2 teaspoon salt
2 tablespoons butter or
   margarine, melted
1/4 cup evaporated milk
4 tablespoons grated Swiss
   cheese
3 eggs, separated
3 tablespoons Italian parsley,
   chopped

*In a large bowl, mix the pumpkin with salt, butter, milk, cheese and beaten egg yolks. Fold in the stiffly-beaten egg whites. Pour into a buttered 9x13 inch baking pan. Sprinkle with Italian parsley. Bake the soufflé at 375 degrees for 25 minutes or until done. **Serves 4-6**.*

Stir-Fried Cabbage with Tomato
(Refogado de Repolho com Tomate)

2 tablespoons olive oil
1 small yellow onion, chopped
4 cloves garlic, crushed
1 small green cabbage,
    shredded
1 sweet red bell pepper, cut
    into 1-inch cubes
4 tablespoons Italian parsley,
    chopped
2 red tomatoes, chopped
1 teaspoon salt
1 teaspoon ground white
    pepper

Heat the oil in a large frying pan and sauté the onion and garlic until golden brown. Add the cabbage, bell pepper, parsley, tomatoes, salt and pepper. Stir-fry for 4 minutes or until the cabbage is tender.
Serves 4-6.

71

Stir-Fried String Beans and Carrots

(Refogado de Vagens e Cenouras)

4 tablespoons vegetable oil
(See page 167.)
1 small yellow onion, chopped
4 cloves garlic, crushed
1 lb. carrots, peeled, thinly
sliced
1 lb. fresh string beans, cut
into 1-inch lengths
1 teaspoon salt
1 teaspoon ground white
pepper
2 tablespoons Italian parsley,
chopped

Heat the oil in a large frying pan and sauté the onion and garlic until golden brown. Add the carrots, beans, salt, pepper and parsley. Stir-fry for 4 minutes or until the vegetables are tender. **Serves 4-6**.

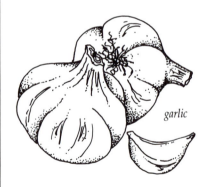

garlic

Stuffed Cabbage with Ground Beef

(Repolho Recheado com Carne Moida de Vaca)

1 quart water
1 large cabbage, washed
1 egg, beaten
1 small yellow onion, chopped
3 cloves garlic, minced
1 lb. lean ground beef
1/2 cup cooked long grain white rice
1 teaspoon ground white pepper
1 teaspoon salt
2 large tomatoes, peeled, chopped
1 can tomato sauce (15 oz.)
1 teaspoon dried oregano

Bring the water to a boil in a deep pot. Plunge the cabbage into boiling water. Boil gently for 2 to 3 minutes. Use a slotted spoon to remove cabbage from the water. Carefully remove outer leaves. Repeat 2 to 3 times or until all the leaves have been removed. Discard the water. In a medium bowl, combine the egg, onion, garlic, beef, rice, pepper and salt. Spread stuffing over each leaf, leaving a 1-inch border uncovered around edges. Roll leaves, enclosing stuffing. Place in a 9x13 inch baking pan and pour the tomatoes and tomato sauce over the cabbage. Sprinkle with oregano. Preheat the oven at 350 degrees for 5 minutes. Bake the cabbage, covered, at 350 degrees for 30 minutes or until the cabbage is cooked.
Serves 6-8.

Stuffed Eggplant

(Beringela Recheada)

2 cups water
1 large eggplant, washed
2 tablespoons butter or
  margarine
1 small yellow onion, chopped
2 cloves garlic, crushed
1 cup fresh mushrooms,
  chopped
1/2 teaspoon salt
1 teaspoon pepper
1 tablespoon Italian parsley,
  chopped
4 tablespoons bread crumbs
4 tablespoons cooked ham,
  chopped (optional)
1 hard boiled egg, chopped
4 tablespoons grated
  Parmesan cheese

Bring the water to a boil in a deep pot. Put the eggplant into the boiling water for 3 minutes. Drain the water and cut the eggplant lengthwise. Remove the eggplant pulp down to about 1/2 inch. Put the pulp aside. Melt the butter in a frying pan and sauté the onion and garlic until light golden brown. Add the eggplant pulp, mushrooms, salt, pepper, parsley, bread crumbs and ham. Stuff the eggplant shells with the mixture and place into a 9x13 inch baking dish and sprinkle with eggs and cheese. Bake the eggplant at 350 degrees for 20 minutes or until the eggplant is tender. **Serves 4.**

Stuffed Green Peppers

(Pimentão Recheado)

1/2 lb. ground pork
1 cup cooked rice
1/2 teaspoon salt
1 small yellow onion, chopped
3 cloves garlic, crushed
4 tablespoons cooked ham,
  chopped
1 teaspoon ground black
  pepper
1 egg, beaten
4 large green bell peppers,
  seeded, cut lengthwise
1 can tomato sauce (15 oz.)

In a bowl, mix the pork, rice, salt, onion, garlic, ham, pepper and egg. Stuff the peppers with this mixture and place into a 9x13 inch baking pan and pour the tomato sauce over the peppers. Preheat the oven at 350 degrees for 5 minutes, then bake the peppers, covered, at 350 degrees for 30 minutes or until the peppers are cooked. **Serves 6-8**.

Stuffed Onions
(Cebolas Recheada)

6 large onions, peeled
1/2 cup water
2 tablespoons butter or
    margarine
2 tablespoons white flour
1 teaspoon salt
1 teaspoon ground white
    pepper
4 tablespoons Italian parsley,
    chopped
2 large tomatoes, peeled,
    chopped
1 cup cooked baby shrimp
1 teaspoon white wine
4 tablespoons bread crumbs
4 tablespoons grated
  Parmesan cheese

In a deep pot, simmer the onions in water at a low temperature for 3 minutes or until slightly soft. Drain. Make a cavity in each onion for the stuffing, reserving pulp. Chop the pulp from the onions. Melt the butter in a frying pan and sauté the chopped onion pulp, flour, salt, pepper, parsley, tomatoes, shrimp and wine for 3 minutes or until thick. Stuff the onions with this mixture and place into a 9x13 inch baking pan and sprinkle with bread crumbs and Parmesan cheese. Bake the onions at 375 degrees for 20 minutes or until tender. **Serves 6-8**.

CHAPTER SIX

SEAFOOD

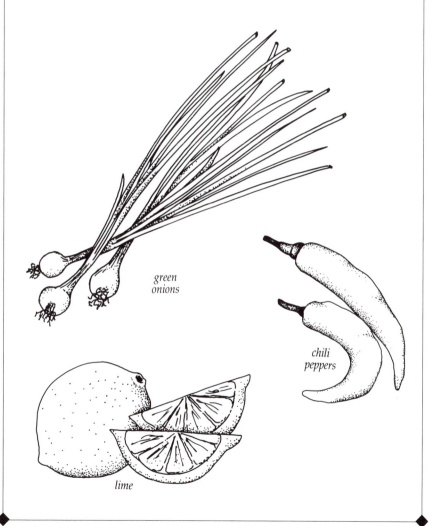

*green
onions*

*chili
peppers*

lime

CHAPTER SIX

Seafood

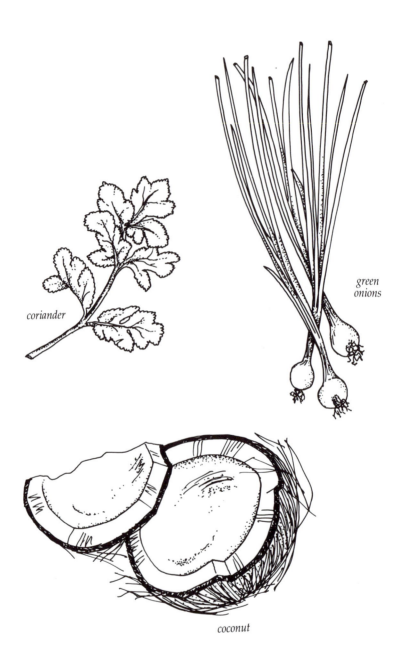

coriander

green onions

coconut

Bahian Fish Muqueca

(Muqueca de Peixe)

4 tablespoons dendê oil
1 yellow onion, finely chopped
1 fresh red hot cayenne
    pepper, chopped
3 cloves garlic, crushed
2 teaspoons ground coriander
2 lbs. halibut, cut into 4-inch
    squares
1/2 teaspoon salt
4 tablespoons fresh lemon
    juice
4 large tomatoes, peeled,
    seeded, chopped
1 teaspoon ground white
    pepper
1 can coconut milk (14 fl. oz.)
2 teaspoons Italian parsley,
    finely chopped

Heat the oil in a medium-sized pot and stir-fry the onion until golden brown. Add the cayenne, garlic, coriander and halibut. Stir-fry for 3 minutes. Add the salt, lemon juice, tomatoes, white pepper, coconut milk and parsley. Simmer for 10 minutes or until the fish is cooked. Serve with Brazilian Rice (See page 124.). **Serves 4-6.**

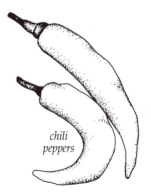

chili peppers

Baked Cod Fish

(Bacalhoada)

2 lbs. dried cod fish
4 cups water
2 lbs. potatoes, peeled,
　　boiled, cut in half
1 cup green olives, pitted
8 tomatoes, peeled, chopped
3 hard boiled eggs, cut in half
3 large yellow onions, sliced
5 green bell peppers, seeded,
　　sliced
1/4 cup olive oil
1 teaspoon ground black
　　pepper

In a bowl, soak the cod fish in some water overnight. Drain, remove bones, and cut in 2-inch squares. In a large pot, bring the water to a boil, then add the cod fish and boil for 3 minutes. Discard the water. In a large baking dish, arrange the cod fish, potatoes, green olives, tomatoes, eggs, onions and peppers in layers. Drizzle with the olive oil and sprinkle with the black pepper. Bake in a 350 degree oven for 40 minutes. **Serves 4-6.**

Cod Fish Soufflé

(Soufflé de Bacalhau)

1 lb. dried cod fish
2 tablespoons olive oil
1 small onion, finely chopped
4 tablespoons Italian parsley
1 small tomato, chopped
2 large potatoes, boiled,
   mashed
1/2 cup milk
4 tablespoons grated
   Parmesan cheese
3 eggs, separated
4 tablespoons bread crumbs

In a bowl, soak the cod fish in water overnight. Drain, remove bones, and cut in 2-inch squares. Heat the oil in a large frying pan and sauté the onion, parsley and tomato for 3 minutes. Add the potatoes, milk, cheese and beaten yolks. Mix well and fold in stiffly-beaten egg whites. Place the mixture in a buttered baking dish and sprinkle with bread crumbs. Bake in a 375 degree oven for 30 minutes or until brown. **Serves 4-6**.

Cod Fish with Beer

(Peixe Assado com Cerveja)

2 lbs. cod fish
1 large onion, finely chopped
4 tablespoons Italian parsley,
  chopped
1 teaspoon ground coriander
3 cloves garlic, crushed
1 red cayenne pepper
juice of 1 lemon
1/2 teaspoon salt
1 teaspoon ground black
  pepper
2 tablespoons olive oil
1/4 cup beer

In a large bowl, marinate the cod fish with onion, parsley, coriander, garlic, pepper, lemon juice, salt, black pepper, olive oil and beer. Let marinate at least one hour, turning the fish so that both sides can absorb the marinade. Place the fish in a baking dish and pour the marinade over it. Bake in a 375 degree oven for 30 minutes or until the fish is cooked. Serve hot. **Serves 4-6**.

Dried Cod Fish

(Refogado de Bacalhau)

1 lb. dried cod fish
2 tablespoons white flour
4 tablespoons olive oil
1 large onion, finely chopped
1 tablespoon Italian parsley,
   chopped
2 cups milk
1 teaspoon ground white
   pepper

In a bowl, soak the cod fish in water overnight. Drain, remove skin and bones, and cut in 2-inch squares. Coat the cod fish squares with flour and set aside for 5 minutes. In a large frying pan with oil, fry the onion and parsley until golden and remove from oil. In the same oil, sauté the cod fish until golden brown. Add the fried onion, parsley, milk and pepper. Simmer, covered, at a low temperature for about 1 hour or until the milk is absorbed. **Serves 4-6**.

Fish and Shrimp Vatapá

(Vatapá de Peixe e Camarão)

4 tablespoons dendê oil

1 yellow onion, finely chopped

1 malagueta or red cayenne
   pepper, chopped

3 cloves garlic, crushed

1 lb. fresh large shrimp,
   shelled, deveined
   (See diagram, page 163.)

2 lbs. seabass, cut into 2-inch
   strips

1/2 cup dried ground shrimp

4 fresh tomatoes, peeled,
   seeded, chopped

1/2 cup ground peanuts,
   roasted

1/2 cup ground cashew nuts

1 teaspoon salt

1 teaspoon ground black
   pepper

1 can coconut milk (14 fl. oz.)

4 tablespoons fresh coriander,
   chopped

Heat the oil in a medium-sized pot and sauté the onion, malagueta and garlic until golden brown. Add the shrimp and seabass and stir-fry for 3 minutes. Add the ground shrimp, tomatoes, peanuts, cashew nuts, salt, pepper and coconut milk. Simmer for 10 minutes or until the fish is cooked. Garnish with coriander leaves. Serve with Brazilian Rice and Coconut Milk (See page 124.).
Serves 6-8.

chili
peppers

Fried Fish

(Peixe Frito)

2 lbs. fillet of flounder
2 tablespoons fresh lemon
  juice
1/2 teaspoon salt
1 teaspoon ground white
  pepper
1 teaspoon ground coriander
4 tablespoons white flour
1/2 cup vegetable oil
  (See page 167.)

Cut the fillet in 2-inch squares and place in a large bowl with lemon juice, salt, pepper and coriander. Let stand for at least 15 minutes. On a platter, coat the squares with flour on both sides. Heat the oil in a frying pan over a medium-high temperature and fry the squares until golden brown on both sides. Remove and drain on paper towels. **Serves 4-6.**

Grilled Grouper

(Peixe Grelhado)

2 lbs. grouper or seabass, cut
  into 4 pieces
1/2 teaspoon salt
1 clove garlic, crushed
3 tablespoons cornstarch
1/4 cup olive oil
1 red cayenne pepper, sliced
1 green cayenne pepper, sliced
 juice of 1 lemon

Season the fish with salt and garlic in a small bowl. Coat with cornstarch on both sides. In a large frying pan with oil, fry the fish until golden brown on both sides. Add the peppers and stir for 2 minutes. Sprinkle with lemon juice. **Serves 4.**

Marinated Fish

(Escabeche de Peixe)

2 lbs. seabass, cut into 2-inch
squares
1/2 teaspoon salt
2 cloves garlic, crushed
1 teaspoon ground white
pepper
juice of 1 lemon
1/2 cup vegetable oil (See
page 167.)
2 large onions, sliced
2 tablespoons olive oil
1 bay leaf
5 large tomatoes, peeled,
chopped
juice of 1 lime
1/2 cup white vinegar

Place the fish, salt, garlic, pepper and lemon juice in a large bowl. Let stand for at least 15 minutes. Heat the oil in a large frying pan and fry the fish until golden brown on both sides. In a separate pan, sauté the onions in olive oil until brown and add the bay leaf, tomatoes, lime juice and vinegar. Bring to a boil, then simmer for 3 minutes. In a baking dish, alternate layers of fish and layers of sauce. Cool uncovered, then cover and store in the refrigerator. Serve cold.
Serves 4-6.

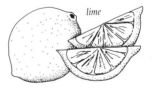

lime

Stuffed Baked Fish

(Peixe Assado com Recheio)

1 whole red snapper or
  grouper (3-4 lbs.)
juice of 2 lemons
1 teaspoon salt
1 lb. baby shrimp, cooked
2 cloves garlic, crushed
1 small onion, finely chopped
4 tablespoons Italian parsley,
  chopped
1 large tomato, chopped
1 teaspoon ground black
  pepper
2 slices of bread, cut into
  cubes
4 tablespoons olive oil
1/2 cup white wine

*Place the fish in a large bowl and rub with lemon juice and salt. Set aside. In a small bowl, mix the shrimp, garlic, onion, parsley, tomato, pepper and bread. Stuff the fish with the shrimp mixture and place in a buttered baking dish. Brush with olive oil and pour the wine over the fish. Bake in a 375 degree oven for 50 minutes or until the fish is cooked. **Serves 4-6.***

Bahian Shrimp Muqueca

(Muqueca de Camarão)

2 tablespoons dendê oil

1 large yellow onion, finely chopped

3 cloves garlic, crushed

2 lbs. fresh medium-sized prawns, shelled, deveined (See diagram, page 163.)

1/2 teaspoon salt

2 tablespoons fresh lemon juice

4 large tomatoes, peeled, seeded, chopped

2 tablespoons Italian parsley, chopped

1 teaspoon black pepper

1 fresh red hot cayenne pepper

1 can coconut milk (14 fl. oz.)

Heat the oil in a medium-sized pot and stir-fry the onion until golden brown. Add the garlic and prawns. Stir-fry for 3 minutes. Add the salt, lemon juice, tomatoes, parsley, pepper, cayenne and coconut milk. Simmer for 5 minutes. Serve with Brazilian Rice with Coconut Milk (See page 124.). **Serves 4-5.**

Bahian Spinach and Dried Shrimp

(Efó)

2 tablespoons dendê oil
1 small yellow onion, chopped
2 cloves garlic, crushed
1/2 teaspoon salt
1 lb. dried ground shrimp
1/2 cup coconut milk
4 pkgs. frozen spinach (10 oz. each), defrosted, drained

Heat the oil in a medium-sized pot and sauté the onion until golden brown. Add the garlic, salt and shrimp. Stir-fry for 2 minutes, then add the coconut milk and spinach. Simmer for 5 minutes, stirring constantly until it forms a smooth paste. Serve with Brazilian Rice and Coconut Milk (See page 124.). **Serves 6-8.**

onions

Deep-Fried Shrimp and NavyBeans

(Acarajé)

2 cups navy beans, washed,
  soaked overnight, drained
1 small yellow onion, chopped
1 cup ground dried shrimp
1/2 teaspoon salt
1 teaspoon ground black
  pepper
1 1/2 cups dendê oil for
  deep-frying

In a blender, mince the beans and onion into a paste. Add the ground dried shrimp, salt and black pepper. Mix well. Heat the oil to a high temperature in a wok. Drop tablespoonfuls of the mixture into the oil and deep-fry until golden brown. Remove and drain on paper towels. Cut the fritters in half and fill with Dried Shrimp Sauce (See page 17.). Serve hot. **Serves 6-8**.

Mashed Potato Pie with Shrimp

(Torta de Camarão)

5 cups mashed potatoes
2 tablespoons white flour
2 eggs, beaten
4 tablespoons grated
  Parmesan cheese
1 teaspoon ground white
  pepper
1/4 teaspoon ground nutmeg
2 tablespoons vegetable oil
  (See page 167.)
1 small yellow onion, chopped
3 cloves garlic, crushed
1 lb. medium shrimp, shelled,
  deveined (See diagram,
  page 163.)
1/4 teaspoon salt
4 tablespoons Italian parsley,
  chopped
12 green pitted olives,
  chopped
2 hard boiled eggs, sliced
1 yolk, beaten

*In a large bowl, combine the potatoes, flour, eggs, Parmesan cheese, pepper and nutmeg. Line a buttered 9x13 inch baking pan with half of the mixture, leaving the rest for the top crust. Heat the oil in a frying pan and sauté the onion until golden brown. Add the garlic, shrimp, salt, Italian parsley and olives. Stir-fry for 3 minutes. Pour over the layer of the potato mixture and arrange the sliced eggs on top. Cover with the remaining potato mixture and brush with the yolk. Bake in a preheated oven at 375 degrees for about 30 minutes or until brown. **Serves 4-6.***

Shrimp Casserole

(Pudim de Camarão)

4 tablespoons vegetable oil
  (See page 167.)
1 small yellow onion, chopped
2 lbs. medium shrimp, shelled,
  deveined (See diagram,
  page 163.)
2 cups mashed potatoes
1/2 teaspoon salt
1/2 teaspoon ground white
  pepper
4 tablespoons grated
  Parmesan cheese
3 tablespoons cornstarch
2 cups milk
1/2 cup bread crumbs
2 tablespoons Italian parsley,
  chopped

Heat the oil in a medium-sized pan and sauté the onion and shrimp until light golden brown. Add the potatoes, salt, pepper, Parmesan cheese, cornstarch and milk. Stir well until it forms a smooth paste. Pour slowly into a buttered 9x13 inch baking pan and sprinkle with bread crumbs and Italian parsley. Bake in a preheated oven at 350 degrees for about 30 minutes or until brown. **Serves 6-8**.

Chayote Squash

(Camarão com Chuchu)

4 tablespoons olive oil
1 small yellow onion, chopped
3 cloves garlic, crushed
1 lb. medium shrimp, shelled,
  deveined (See diagram,
  page 163.)
4 large chayote squash, peeled,
  sliced
2 tomatoes, peeled, chopped
1/2 teaspoon salt
1/2 teaspoon ground white
  pepper
1 can coconut milk (14 fl. oz.)

Heat the oil in a medium-sized pan and sauté the onion until light golden brown. Add the garlic and shrimp. Stir-fry for 3 minutes and add the squash, tomatoes, salt, pepper and coconut milk. Simmer for 10 minutes or until chayote squash is tender. Serve with Brazilian Rice and Coconut Milk (See page 124.).
Serves 4-6.

shallots

Shrimp with Cheese

(Camarão com Queijo)

2 tablespoons dendê oil
1 large yellow onion, chopped
1/2 teaspoon salt
2 lbs. medium shrimp, shelled,
   deveined (See diagram,
   page 163.)
2 tablespoons fine corn meal
2 cups milk
1 cup grated Parmesan cheese
4 egg whites
1/2 cup bread crumbs
4 tablespoons grated
   Parmesan cheese
4 tablespoons Italian parsley,
   chopped

Heat the oil in a medium-sized pan and sauté the onion, salt and shrimp until light golden brown. Add the corn meal, milk and 1 cup of Parmesan cheese. Cook until thick. Pour into a buttered 9x13 inch baking pan and cover with stiffly-beaten egg whites. Sprinkle with bread crumbs, the rest of the Parmesan cheese and parsley. Bake in a preheated oven at 375 degrees for about 30 minutes or until brown. **Serves 6-8.**

Crab Soufflé

(Soufflé de Caranquejos)

2 tablespoons butter or
  margarine
1 small onion, finely chopped
1/2 teaspoon salt
1 teaspoon ground white
  pepper
2 tablespoons white flour
2 large tomatoes, peeled,
  chopped
1 cup milk
1 cup canned crab meat
3 eggs, separated
4 tablespoons grated
  Parmesan cheese

Melt the butter in a large frying pan and sauté the onion until light brown. Add the salt, pepper, flour, tomatoes, milk, crab meat and beaten egg yolks. Mix well and fold in stiffly-beaten egg whites. Pour into a buttered 9x13 inch baking pan and sprinkle with Parmesan cheese. Bake in a preheated oven at 375 degrees for about 30 minutes or until brown. **Serves 4-6.**

Stuffed Crabs

(Caranguejos Recheados)

2 tablespoons butter or
  margarine
1 small onion, finely chopped
2 tablespoons flour
2/3 cup milk
1/2 teaspoon salt
juice of 1 lemon
1 teaspoon ground white
  pepper
2 tablespoons white wine
2 cups canned crab meat
2 tablespoons Italian parsley,
  chopped
1/2 cup bread crumbs
6 crab shells or individual
  4-inch diameter baking
  dishes

*Melt the butter in a large frying pan and sauté the onion until golden brown. Add the flour and mix well. Add the milk, salt, lemon juice, pepper, wine, crab meat and parsley. Cook for 3 minutes or until thick. Fill crab shells or individual 4-inch diameter baking dishes. Sprinkle bread crumbs over the filled shells. Bake in a 425 degree oven for 15 minutes. **Serves 6.***

CHAPTER SEVEN

MEAT
&
POULTRY

coriander
or cilantro

mint

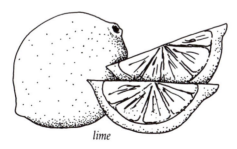

lime

CHAPTER SEVEN
Meat and Poultry

garlic

chili
peppers

. shallots

Beef Cooked in Beer

(Bife com Cerveja)

2 tablespoons olive oil
2 lbs. sirloin steak, cut into 1
   inch cubes
1/2 teaspoon salt
1 teaspoon ground black
   pepper
1 cup light beer
1 large onion, sliced
1 tablespoon tomato paste

Heat the oil in a large frying pan and sauté the beef with salt and pepper for 3 minutes or until both sides are brown. Add the beer, onion and tomato paste. Cook over low heat for 30 minutes or until the meat is tender.
Serves 4-6.

Beef with Onion

(Bife Acebolado)

1 lb. beef tenderloin, thinly
   sliced
4 cloves garlic, crushed
1/4 teaspoon salt
1/2 teaspoon ground black
   pepper
4 tablespoons olive oil
1 large yellow onion, thinly
   sliced
1 lime, cut into 4 wedges

In a bowl, thoroughly mix the beef, garlic, salt and black pepper. Marinate the beef for at least 1 hour or overnight, refrigerated. Heat the oil in a large frying pan and stir-fry the beef and onion until light brown. Garnish with lime. **Serves 2-4.**

Brazilian Meat Balls

(Almôndegas)

1 lb. lean ground beef
3 cloves garlic, crushed
1 small onion, finely chopped
4 tablespoons Italian parsley,
 chopped
1/2 teaspoon salt
1/2 teaspoon ground black
 pepper
1 egg, beaten
1/2 cup olive oil for frying
1 cup tomato sauce
2 bay leaves
4 tablespoons white wine

In a large bowl, mix well the beef, garlic, onion, parsley, salt, pepper and egg. Shape into small balls 1-inch in diameter. Fry in olive oil. Drain on absorbent paper. Set aside. Put the tomato sauce, bay leaves and wine in a deep pot and add the fried meat balls. Simmer for 15 minutes. **Serves 4.**

Ground Beef with Herbs

(Picadinho de Carne)

2 tablespoons vegetable oil
(See page 167.)

1 small yellow onion, chopped

4 cloves garlic, crushed

2 lbs. extra lean ground beef

4 tablespoons Italian parsley,
chopped

4 tablespoons green onion,
chopped

1/2 teaspoon salt

2 large tomatoes, peeled,
chopped

2 hard boiled eggs, chopped

1 cup pitted green olives,
chopped

Heat the oil in a large frying pan and sauté the onion until golden brown. Add the garlic and ground beef. Stir-fry for 5 minutes. Add the Italian parsley, green onion, salt and tomatoes. Simmer for 3 minutes or until the beef is cooked. Garnish with eggs and green olives. **Serves 6-8.**

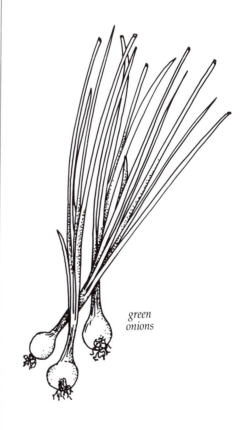

green onions

Pot Roast with Bacon

(Carne de Vaca com Bacon)

1 tablespoon vegetable oil
(See page 167.)
1/4 lb. bacon, chopped
4 cloves garlic, crushed
2 large onions, sliced
4 lb. chuck roast
1/2 teaspoon salt
1 teaspoon ground black
  pepper
2 bay laurel leaves

Heat the oil in a large deep pot and stir-fry the bacon for 3 minutes. Add the garlic, onions, beef, salt, pepper and bay leaves and brown the meat on both sides. Cover and cook over low heat for 2 hours or until the meat is tender. *Serves 6-8.*

Pot Roast with Oranges

(Carne de Vaca com Laranja)

4 lb. chuck roast
juice of 1 lemon
1 teaspoon salt
4 cloves garlic, crushed
4 tablespoons olive oil
2 small onions, chopped
4 small tomatoes, peeled,
  chopped
2 bay laurel leaves
1 teaspoon ground black
  pepper
2 cups fresh orange juice

In a large bowl, season the beef with lemon juice, salt and garlic. Set aside. Heat the oil in a large deep pot and stir-fry the onion and beef until golden brown. Add the tomatoes, bay leaves, pepper and orange juice. Cover and cook over low heat for 1 hour or until the meat is tender. *Serves 6-8.*

Stewed Steak

(Bifes Ensopados)

2 lbs. round steak, cut into
  1 inch cubes
1 teaspoon ground black
  pepper
1/2 teaspoon salt
4 cloves garlic, crushed
2 tablespoons vegetable oil
  (See page 167.)
1 large onion, sliced
6 tablespoons Italian parsley,
  chopped
1 cup port wine

In a small bowl, season the steak with pepper, salt and garlic on both sides. Let stand for 10 minutes. Heat the oil in a deep pot and stir-fry the steak on both sides until brown. Add the onions, parsley and wine. Cover and simmer for about 1 hour or until the meat is tender. **Serves 4-6.**

Stir-Fried Tenderloin with Carrots

(Refogado de Carne com Cenoura)

2 tablespoons olive oil
3 cloves garlic, crushed
1 large onion, sliced
1 lb. tenderloin beef, thinly
  sliced
1 large carrot, cut into julienne
  strips
1/2 teaspoon salt
1 teaspoon ground black
  pepper
2 tablespoons fresh lemon
  juice

Heat the oil in a medium-sized pot and sauté the garlic and onion until light golden brown. Add the beef and stir-fry for 2 minutes. Add the carrots, salt, pepper and lemon juice. Stir-fry for 2 more minutes or until the carrots are tender. **Serves 4-6.**

Stuffed Beef Roll

(Carne Enrolada)

2 pieces, 1 1/2 lbs. each, flank
  steak, partially frozen,
  1 inch thick
6 cloves garlic, crushed
1 teaspoon salt
1 teaspoon ground black
  pepper
1/2 cup Italian parsley,
  chopped
2 large carrots, cut into
  quarters lengthwise
2 hard boiled eggs, cut in
  wedges
1 large onion, cut in rings
6 slices bacon, fried
1/4 cup pitted green olives
2 tablespoons vegetable oil
  (See page 167.)
1 teaspoon dried thyme
1/2 cup white wine
1 can tomato paste (12 oz.)
2 cups water
kitchen string

Cut each piece of the flank steak down the middle lengthwise so that it opens like a book. (See diagram, page 164.) In a small bowl, mix the garlic, salt, pepper and Italian parsley. Rub both pieces of meat with the mixture, inside and out. Marinate for at least 1 hour or overnight, refrigerated. Next, lay each piece of the meat on a flat surface, open like a book, and arrange the carrots, eggs, onion, bacon and olives in rows. Roll the pieces tightly. After they are rolled, secure the pieces with kitchen string so that they do not open while cooking. Heat the oil in a deep pot, then fry the meat until golden brown on both sides. Add the thyme, wine, tomato paste and water. Cover the pot and cook at low temperature for 1 hour or until the meat is tender. Remove the meat and reserve sauce. Cool. Remove the string and cut the meat in slices. Before serving, pour the reserved sauce over the sliced meat. **Serves 6-8.**

Tenderloin Beef with Farofa

(Bife com Farofa)

2 tablespoons olive oil
2 lbs. tenderloin beef, thinly
    sliced
4 tablespoons fresh lime juice
1 teaspoon salt
3 cloves garlic, crushed
6 tablespoons Italian parsley,
    chopped

In a bowl, thoroughly mix the oil, beef, lime juice, salt, garlic and Italian parsley. Marinate the beef for at least 1 hour or overnight, refrigerated. Grill until lightly browned. Serve with Brazilian Rice (See page 124.), Manioc Meal with Butter and Egg (See page 18.) and Vinaigrette Sauce (See page 20.).
Serves 4-6.

Breaded Veal Cutlet

(Bife à Milanesa)

2 lbs. veal steak, 1/2 inch
   thick individual servings
4 cloves garlic, crushed
1 teaspoon salt
1 teaspoon ground white
   pepper
2 tablespoons Italian parsley,
   chopped
4 eggs, beaten
2 cups fine bread crumbs
1/2 cup vegetable oil for deep-
   frying (See page 167.)

Rub each piece of steak on both sides with garlic, salt, pepper and Italian parsley. Dip each piece of steak in the egg and then coat the steaks with bread crumbs. Deep-fry the breaded meat in a large frying pan over medium heat for about 3 minutes on each side or until golden brown. Serve with Pepper and Lemon Sauce (See page 20.). (The same recipe can be used for beef, chicken, fish or shrimp.)
Serves 4-6.

Roast Leg of Lamb

(Perna de Carneiro Assada)

1 cup dry white wine
6 cloves garlic, crushed
1 red cayenne pepper
1 teaspoon salt
1 teaspoon ground black
   pepper
4 tablespoons fresh mint,
   chopped
6 tablespoons Italian parsley,
   chopped
1 large onion, finely chopped
4-6 lb. leg of lamb

In a large bowl, mix the wine, garlic, cayenne, salt, pepper, mint, parsley and onion. Add the lamb and marinate for at least 1 hour or overnight, refrigerated. Put the lamb in a large roasting pan and pour the mixture over it. Bake, covered, about 2 hours in a preheated oven at 350 degrees. Uncover and bake for 30 more minutes or until the top is brown.
Serves 6-8.

mint

Roast Leg of Pork

(Pernil de Porco)

1 cup dry white wine
4 tablespoons fresh lime juice
6 cloves garlic, crushed
3 bay leaves
2 tablespoons Italian parsley,
  chopped
2 large onions, sliced
1 teaspoon ground black
  pepper
1 red cayenne pepper
1 teaspoon salt
2 green bell peppers, sliced
1 red bell pepper, sliced
4-6 lb. leg of pork

In a large bowl, mix the wine, lime , garlic, bay leaves, Italian parsley, onion, pepper, cayenne, salt, green and red bell peppers. Add the pork and marinate for at least 1 hour or overnight, refrigerated. Place the pork in a large roasting pan and pour the mixture over it. Bake, covered, about 2 hours in a preheated oven at 350 degrees. Uncover and bake for 30 more minutes or until the top is brown.
Serves 6-8.

Brazilian Orange Duck

(Pato Assado com Laranja)

1 cup white wine
4 cloves garlic, crushed
juice of 1 lime
1 tablespoon green onion, chopped
2 tablespoons Italian parsley, chopped
1 teaspoon salt
1 teaspoon ground white pepper
4 lb. whole young duck
juice of 2 oranges

In a bowl, combine the wine, garlic, lime juice, green onion, Italian parsley, salt and pepper. Pour over the duck and marinate for at least 1 hour or overnight, refrigerated. Bake, uncovered, at 375 degrees for 1 hour or until the duck is tender and golden brown on both sides, basting occasionally with orange juice. **Serves 6-8.**

Chicken Curry

(Frango ao Molho Curry)

2 tablespoons vegetable oil
(See page 167.)
1 yellow onion, chopped
4 cloves garlic, crushed
4 large tomatoes, peeled, finely
chopped
1 teaspoon salt
1 tablespoon ground coriander
1 teaspoon ground cumin
1 tablespoon curry powder
2 whole chicken breasts,
boned, skinned, cut into
2-inch cubes
1 can coconut milk (14 fl. oz.)
1 cup sour cream

Heat the oil in a medium-sized pot and stir-fry the onion and garlic until brown. Add the tomatoes, salt, coriander, cumin, curry powder and chicken and stir for 1 minute. Simmer for about 20 minutes over low heat or until the chicken is tender. Add the coconut milk and sour cream and simmer again for 3 more minutes. Serve with Brazilian Rice (See page 124.). **Serves 4-6.**

Chicken Pie with Palm Heart

(Torta de Frango e Palmito)

Filling

2 tablespoons butter or
  margarine
2 cloves garlic, minced
1 large onion, finely chopped
2 cups cooked chicken breast,
  skinned, cubed
2 tablespoons Italian parsley,
  chopped
2 tablespoons white flour
1 teaspoon salt
1/2 teaspoon ground white
  pepper
2 tablespoons ketchup
1 cup chopped palm heart
1/4 cup milk
2 hard boiled eggs, sliced
1/4 cup green olives, sliced

Crust

2 1/2 cups white flour, sifted
1/4 teaspoon salt
1/2 cup butter or margarine
3 egg yolks

Melt the butter in a deep pot and sauté the garlic and onion until brown. Add the chicken, parsley, flour, salt, pepper, ketchup, palm heart and milk and stir well for 2 minutes or until the mixture is creamy. Let cool. In a large bowl, make the crust by mixing well the flour, salt, butter and 2 yolks. Divide dough into 2 equal portions. Roll 1 portion into a 12-inch circle. Place in a 9-inch pie pan and fill with the chicken mixture, then layer the sliced eggs and olives on top. Roll out the remaining dough into a 10-inch circle and place over the filling. Fold the upper crust under the lower crust to make a raised edge. Brush with 1 beaten yolk. Bake in a 350 degree oven for 30 minutes or until the top of the pie is light golden brown. **Serves 4-6.**

Chicken Vatapá

(Vatapá de Frango)

2 tablespoons dendê oil
1 yellow onion, finely chopped
2 fresh cayenne peppers,
   chopped
3 cloves garlic, crushed
3-4 lbs. boneless chicken
   breasts, skinned, cut into
   2-inch cubes
4 fresh tomatoes, peeled,
   seeded, chopped
1/2 cup dried ground shrimp
1/2 cup ground peanuts,
   roasted
1/2 cup ground cashew nuts
4 tablespoons Italian parsley,
   finely chopped
1 teaspoon salt
1/2 teaspoon ground black
   pepper
1 can coconut milk (14 fl. oz.)
6 tablespoons fresh coriander
   leaves, chopped

Heat the oil in a medium-sized pot and sauté the onion, cayenne and garlic until light golden brown. Add the chicken and stir-fry for 5 minutes. Add the tomatoes, shrimp, peanuts, cashews, Italian parsley, salt, pepper and coconut milk. Simmer for 20 minutes or until the chicken is tender. Garnish with fresh coriander leaves. Serve with Brazilian Rice with Coconut Milk (See page 124.). **Serves 6-8.**

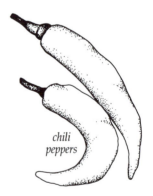

chili peppers

Chicken with Sour Cream

(Fricassé de Frango)

2 tablespoons butter or
   margarine
1 small onion, finely chopped
2 whole chicken breasts,
   boned, skinned, cut into
   1-inch cubes
2 cups mushrooms, sliced
1/2 cup dry white wine
1 teaspoon salt
1 teaspoon ground white
   pepper
2 tablespoons ketchup
2 cups sour cream

Heat the butter in a medium-sized pot and stir-fry the onion until brown. Add the chicken and mushrooms and stir for 3 minutes. Add the wine, salt, pepper and ketchup and simmer for about 20 minutes over low heat or until the chicken is tender. Add the sour cream and simmer again for 3 more minutes. Serve with Brazilian Rice (See page 124.). **Serves 4-6.**

Chicken with White Wine

(Frango com Vinho Branco)

3-4 lbs. drumsticks
3 cloves garlic, crushed
1 teaspoon ground black
   pepper
1 teaspoon salt
4 tablespoons Italian parsley,
   chopped
1 cup white wine
1 small onion, chopped
2 tablespoons olive oil
1 cup tomato sauce

*Marinate the chicken overnight, refrigerated, in garlic, pepper, salt, Italian parsley and wine. The next day, remove from the marinade and stir-fry the chicken and onion in hot olive oil until golden brown on both sides. Add the tomato sauce and the marinade mixture. Cover and cook for 30 minutes or until the chicken is tender. **Serves 4-6**.*

Deep-Fried Chicken with Garlic

(Frango Frito com Alho)

12 drumsticks
4 cloves garlic, crushed
1 teaspoon salt
1 teaspoon ground white
   pepper
juice of 1 lemon
1 egg white
4 tablespoons cornstarch
2 cups vegetable oil for deep-
   frying (See page 167.)

*In a small bowl, combine the drumsticks with garlic, salt, pepper, lemon, egg white and cornstarch. Marinate for 15 minutes. Deep-fry in hot oil until golden brown on both sides. Remove and drain on paper towels. **Serves 4-6**.*

Milk Chicken

(Frango com Leite)

2 tablespoons butter or
  margarine
1 small yellow onion, chopped
3 cloves garlic, crushed
4 lbs. boneless chicken
  breasts, cut into 1-inch cubes
1/2 teaspoon salt
1 teaspoon ground black
  pepper
1 tablespoon Italian parsley,
  chopped
1 bay leaf
3 cups milk

Melt the butter in a medium-sized pan and sauté the onion until light golden brown. Add the garlic, chicken, salt, pepper, Italian parsley and bay leaf. Stir-fry for 3 minutes. Add the milk and cook over low heat until tender. **Serves 6-8.**

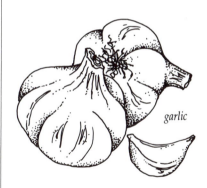

garlic

Roast Chicken

(Frango Assado)

3-4 lb. whole chicken
juice of 1 lemon
1 cup light beer
4 cloves garlic, crushed
2 bay laurel leaves
4 tablespoons Italian parsley,
  chopped
1 teaspoon dried oregano
1 teaspoon salt
1 teaspoon ground white
  pepper

Place the chicken in a large bowl and sprinkle lemon juice in the cavity and on the outside. Add the beer, garlic, bay leaves, Italian parsley, oregano, salt and white pepper. Marinate the chicken for 2 hours, or overnight, refrigerated. Remove the chicken from the marinade, then stuff the neck and stomach cavities with Giblet Stuffing (See page 18.) and close by sewing the skin together over the farofa (Giblet Stuffing). Bake in a 375 degree oven for about 1 hour or until the chicken is tender and golden brown on both sides.
Serves 4.

CHAPTER EIGHT

RICE, BEANS
&
NOODLES

garlic

onions

CHAPTER EIGHT

Rice, Beans and Noodles

Baked Rice with Chicken

(Arroz ao Forno com Frango)

2 tablespoons olive oil
1 small onion, chopped
3 cloves garlic, minced
1 lb. boneless chicken breast,
   cut into 1-inch cubes
2 small tomatoes, peeled,
   chopped
1 tablespoon Italian parsley,
   chopped
2 cups white long grain rice,
   washed, drained
1/2 teaspoon salt
3 cups boiling water
2 hard boiled eggs, sliced
2 cups frozen peas
1 cup green olives
1/2 cup Parmesan cheese

In a 4 quart pot, heat the oil over medium-high heat and stir-fry the onion and garlic until golden. Add the chicken, tomatoes, parsley, rice and salt. Stir for 3 minutes. Add the boiling water and bring to a boil, uncovered, until almost all the water is evaporated. Pour the mixture into a buttered 9x13 inch baking pan and decorate the top with eggs, frozen peas, green olives and Parmesan cheese. Bake, covered, at 350 degrees for 20 minutes.
Serves 4-6.

Brazilian Rice

(Arroz Brasileiro)

4 tablespoons vegetable oil
(See page 167.)
1 yellow onion, finely chopped
3 cloves garlic, crushed
3 cups white long grain rice,
washed, drained
4 cups boiling water
1 bay leaf
2 medium tomatoes, peeled,
seeded, chopped
1/2 teaspoon salt

In a 4 quart pot, heat the oil over medium-high heat and stir-fry the onion and garlic until golden. Pour in the rice and stir for 2 to 3 minutes. Add the water, bay leaf, tomatoes and salt. Return to a boil and continue stirring until almost all the water is evaporated, about 5 minutes. Cover the pot and reduce the temperature. Simmer for 20 minutes or until the rice is cooked. **Serves 4-6.**

Brazilian Rice with Coconut Milk

(Arroz Brasileiro com Leite de Coco)

3 tablespoons vegetable oil
(See page 167.)
1 small yellow onion, finely
chopped
3 cloves garlic, crushed
3 cups white long grain rice,
washed, drained
1/2 teaspoon salt
4 cups boiling water
1 can coconut milk (14 fl. oz.)

Heat the oil in a medium-sized pot and stir-fry the onion and garlic until golden brown. Add the rice, stirring with a wooden spoon, until the rice is hot and coated with oil, about 3 minutes. Add the salt, boiling water and coconut milk. Bring to a boil, uncovered, until the liquid is almost evaporated, about 5 minutes. Cover and simmer about 20 minutes or until the rice is cooked. **Serves 4-6.**

Delicious Rice and Ham

(Arroz com Presunto)

3 tablespoons vegetable oil
  (See page 167.)
1 small yellow onion, chopped
3 cloves garlic, crushed
1/2 teaspoon salt
4 tablespoons Italian parsley,
  chopped
3 large tomatoes, peeled,
  chopped
3 cups white long grain rice,
  washed, drained
1 cup cooked ham, chopped
4 cups boiling water
3 hard boiled eggs, sliced
1/2 cup pitted green olives,
  chopped
1/2 cup Parmesan cheese

*Heat the oil in a deep pot and sauté the onion and garlic until light golden brown. Add the salt, parsley, tomatoes, rice and ham. Stir well. Add the boiling water. Bring to a boil, uncovered, until the liquid is almost evaporated, about 5 minutes. Cover and simmer about 20 minutes or until the rice is cooked. Garnish with eggs, olives and Parmesan cheese. **Serves 4-6.***

Rice with Chicken

(Arroz com Frango)

2 tablespoons vegetable oil
  (See page 167.)
4 slices bacon, chopped
8 drumsticks
6 Italian sausages, cut into 1
  inch pieces
1 small yellow onion, chopped
3 cloves garlic, crushed
1/2 teaspoons salt
2 large tomatoes, peeled,
  chopped
2 tablespoons Italian parsley,
  chopped
1 tablespoon green onion,
  chopped
1 teaspoon ground white
  pepper
3 cups white long grain rice,
  washed, drained
4 cups boiling water

Heat the oil in a deep pot and sauté the bacon, drumsticks and sausage for 3 minutes or until golden brown. Add the onion, garlic and salt. Stir for 2 minutes. Add the tomatoes, parsley, green onion, pepper and rice. Stir well and add the boiling water. Bring to a boil, uncovered, until the liquid is almost evaporated, about 5 minutes. Cover and simmer about 20 minutes or until the rice and meat are cooked.
Serves 6-8.

Brazilian Black Beans

(Feijoada Completa)

2 tablespoons vegetable oil
(See page 167.)

1 large yellow onion, chopped

4 cloves garlic, crushed

4 cups dried black beans,
soaked overnight, drained

1 lb. salt pork, boiled for 5
minutes, cut into 1-inch
cubes

2 lbs. Portuguese sausage
(linguiça) or Italian sausage

1 lb. smoked lean ham hocks

2 lbs. corned beef, cut into
2-inch cubes

1/2 teaspoon salt

2 teaspoons ground black
pepper

4 bay leaves

1 fresh orange, washed very
well, cut in half

2 1/2 quarts water

6 oranges, peeled, sliced

Heat the oil in a large, heavy, deep pot and stir-fry the onion and garlic for 1 minute or until light golden brown. Add the beans, salt pork, Portuguese sausage, ham hocks, corned beef, salt, black pepper, bay leaves, halved-orange and water. Cover and simmer for 2 hours or until the beans are tender, stirring occasionally and adding water if needed. Serve with sliced oranges, Manioc Meal with Butter and Eggs (See page 18.), Brazilian Rice (See page 124.), Collard Greens (See page 66 .), Vinaigrette Sauce (See page 20.) and Cachaça (Brazilian Spirits) Cocktail (See page 160.).
Serves 8-10.

Kidney Beans
(Feijão)

2 tablespoons vegetable oil
  (See page 167.)
1 small yellow onion, chopped
3 cloves garlic, crushed
1 teaspoon ground black
  pepper
2 cups kidney beans, washed,
  soaked overnight, drained
1/4 lb. salt pork, washed,
   drained, cut into 1-inch
   cubes
1 quart water

Heat the oil in a medium-sized pot and sauté the onion and garlic until light golden brown. Add the pepper, beans, salt pork and water. Cook for 2 hours or until the beans are tender. Serve with Brazilian Rice (See page 124.) and Manioc Meal with Butter and Eggs (See page 18.). **Serves 6-8.**

garlic

Vegetarian Black Beans

(Feijão Preto)

2 tablespoons vegetable oil
  (See page 167.)
1 large yellow onion, chopped
4 cloves garlic, crushed
4 cups dried black beans,
  soaked overnight, drained
1/2 teaspoon salt
1/2 teaspoon ground black
  pepper
4 bay leaves
2 quarts water

Heat the oil in a large deep pot and stir-fry the onion and garlic until brown. Add the beans, salt, pepper, bay leaves and water. Cover and cook for one hour or until the beans are tender. Serve with Manioc Meal with Butter and Eggs (See page18.) and Brazilian Rice (See page124.).
Serves 6-8.

White Beans

(Feijão Branco)

2 tablespoons vegetable oil
  (See page 167.)
1 small yellow onion, chopped
3 cloves garlic, crushed
1/2 teaspoon ground black
  pepper
2 cups white beans, washed,
  soaked overnight, drained
1 lb. smoked ham
1 bay leaf
2 tablespoons Italian parsley,
  chopped
1 quart water

Heat the oil in a medium-sized pot and sauté the onion and garlic until golden brown. Add the pepper, beans, ham, bay leaf, Italian parsley and water. Cook for 2 hours or until the beans are tender. Serve with Brazilian Rice (See page 124.). **Serves 6-8.**

shallots

Baked Spaghetti with Ham

(Macarrão ao Forno com Presunto)

1 lb. cooked spaghetti
1/2 lb. cooked ham, thinly
  sliced
1/2 cup green olives, sliced
2 hard boiled eggs, sliced
2 large tomatoes, sliced
1 cup grated Parmesan cheese
2 tablespoons butter or
  margarine
1 large onion, finely chopped
2 cloves garlic, minced
4 tablespoons Italian parsley,
  chopped
1/2 teaspoon salt
4 tablespoons white flour,
  sifted
2 cups milk
4 tablespoons Parmesan
  cheese

In a large buttered casserole dish, arrange alternately in layers the spaghetti, ham, olives, eggs, tomatoes and cheese. Set aside. Melt the butter in a small pan and sauté the onion and garlic until light golden brown. Add the parsley, salt, flour and milk and stir well for 1 minute. Simmer for 3 minutes, stirring occasionally, until the mixture is creamy. Pour this sauce mixture over the spaghetti casserole. Sprinkle with cheese and bake in a 375 degree oven for 20 minutes or until the top is light brown.
Serves 4-6.

Fettuccini with Meat Sauce

(Macarrão com Molho de Carne)

2 tablespoons olive oil
1 onion, finely chopped
4 cloves garlic, minced
1 lb. lean ground beef
4 tablespoons Italian parsley,
  chopped
1/2 teaspoon salt
1 teaspoon ground white
  pepper
6 large tomatoes, peeled,
  seeded, chopped
1 teaspoon dried oregano
2 fresh carrots, grated
2 quarts water
1 lb. egg fettuccini
1/4 cup grated Parmesan
  cheese

Heat the oil in a deep pot and sauté the onions and garlic until light golden brown. Add the beef, parsley, salt and pepper and stir-fry for 2 minutes. Add the tomatoes, oregano and carrots. Cover and simmer for 30 minutes over low heat. Keep warm. In another large pot, bring the water to a boil. Gradually add the fettuccini, being sure the water continues to boil. Stir occasionally. Cook for 8 to 10 minutes or until tender but firm. Drain the noodles. Pour the meat sauce over the cooked noodles. Garnish with Parmesan cheese. **Serves 4.**

CHAPTER NINE

DESSERTS

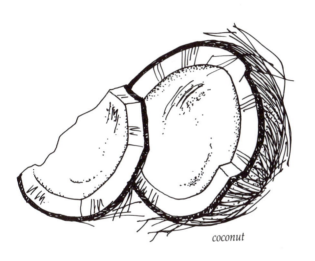

coconut

papaya

Desserts

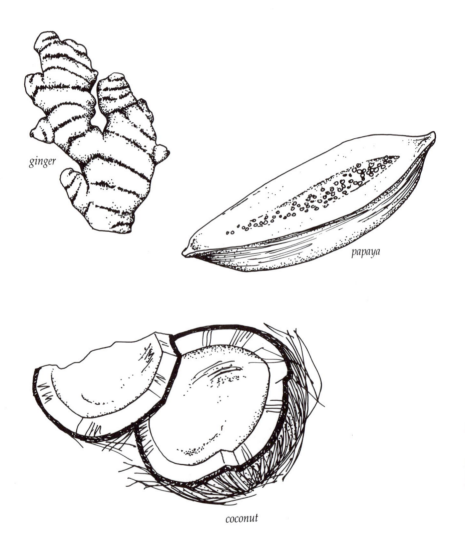

ginger

papaya

coconut

Avocado Cream

(Creme de Abacate)

4 large ripe avocados, peeled,
  seeded
2 tablespoons sugar
1 cup milk

In a blender, blend all the ingredients into a paste. Pour into individual cups with crushed ice. **Serves 4.**

Avocado Ice Cream

(Sorvete de Abacate)

4 ripe avocados, peeled,
  seeded
1 tablespoon fresh lime juice
4 tablespoons sugar
1 pint whipping cream

Blend the avocados, lime juice and sugar in a blender. In a large bowl, combine the avocado mixture with the whipping cream. Put the mixture in an ice cream maker or place the mixture in a pan in the freezer and freeze until it is icy and almost set. Scrape it into a mixing bowl and beat it thoroughly with a wooden spoon, or at low speed with an electric mixer. Return it to the freezer and freeze until it is set. **Serves 4-6.**

Beer Cake

(Bolo de Cerveja)

**4 tablespoons butter or
  margarine
2/3 cup sugar
3 eggs, separated
1 1/2 cups white flour, sifted
1/2 cup flat beer
1 teaspoon baking powder**

*In a bowl, beat the butter
and sugar until creamy, then add
the egg yolks and beat well. Add
the flour and beer alternately and
mix well. Add the baking powder
and fold in stiffly beaten egg
whites. Pour into a buttered 8x8
inch baking pan. Bake in a 350
degree oven for 40 minutes.*
Serves 4-6.

Brazilian Chocolate Nut Squares

(Doce de Chocolate com Nozes)

1 1/2 cups sugar
1 cup whipping cream
1 cup chocolate powder
 (unsweetened cocoa)
2 tablespoons butter or
 margarine
2 cups ground Brazil nuts
1/4 teaspoon salt
1 teaspoon vanilla

In a medium-sized pot, bring the sugar, whipping cream, chocolate and butter to a boil and simmer for 5 minutes. Add the nuts, salt and vanilla. Reduce the temperature to low and continue cooking, stirring constantly, until the mixture pulls away from the sides of the pot. Pour into a buttered 9x13 inch baking pan and press the mixture flat. Cut into 2 inch squares. Let cool before removing from the baking pan. **Makes 20 squares.**

Caramel Custard

(Pudim de Leite)

1/2 cup sugar for caramel
3 eggs, well-beaten
1 can sweetened condensed
   milk   (12 fl. oz.)
1 cup milk or fresh orange
   juice
1 teaspoon vanilla

In a small heavy pan, melt the sugar over a low temperature until it is caramelized. Pour into a 9 inch diameter ring mold, tilting the pan so that the caramel coats the sides well. In a bowl, mix well the eggs, condensed milk, milk (or orange juice) and vanilla. Pour into the mold with the caramelized sugar. Put the mold in a 10x15 inch pan containing 1 inch of hot water and bake in a 350 degree oven for 1 hour or until the custard is set. Cool. Unmold on a large deep plate. Serve cold. **Serves 4-6**.

Chocolate Balls

(Brigadeiros)

1 can sweetened condensed
  milk (12 fl. oz.)
4 tablespoons chocolate
  powder (unsweetened cocoa)
1 tablespoon butter or
  margarine
1/4 teaspoon salt
1 cup chocolate sprinkles

In a medium-sized pan, combine the condensed milk and chocolate powder. Cook over a low temperature, stirring constantly, until the mixture pulls away from the sides of the pan. Add the butter and salt and mix it in thoroughly before removing the mixture from the flame. When cool, make into little balls about 1 inch in diameter and roll in chocolate sprinkles. Place in small paper baking cups.
Makes 20 balls.

Chocolate Nut Squares

(Docinho de Chocolate e Nozes)

2/3 cup sugar
1/2 cup whipping cream
1/4 cup chocolate powder
  (unsweetened cocoa)
1 tablespoon butter
1 cup ground almonds

Bring the sugar, whipping cream, chocolate powder and butter to a boil in a medium-sized pot. Cook for 5 minutes, then add the nuts, stirring constantly until the mixture pulls away from the sides of the pot. Pour into a buttered 9x13 inch baking pan. Let cool. Cut into small squares.
Makes 15 squares.

Coconut and Cheese Cupcake

(Bombocado de Coco e Queijo)

1 cup sugar
1/2 cup water
2 tablespoons butter or
   margarine, melted
1/3 cup white flour, sifted
2 cups fresh coconut, finely
   grated
3 eggs, beaten
2 tablespoons grated
   Parmesan cheese
muffin tins

In a small pan, combine the sugar and water and cook over a low heat, occasionally stirring, until it spins a thread. Add the butter and cool. Mix the flour, coconut, eggs and cheese in a bowl, then add them to the syrup and mix well. Pour into small, buttered and floured individual muffin tins and bake in a 350 degree oven for 30 minutes or until the top is browned.
Makes 12-14.

Coconut and Pineapple Balls

(Doce de Coco e Abacaxi)

2 cans (20 oz. each) pineapple
  chunks, drained
2 cups dried coconut, finely
  grated
2 cups sugar
1 cup crystallized sugar for
  decoration

Blend the pineapple in the blender or food processor until finely minced. In a medium-sized pan, cook the pineapple purée, coconut and sugar, stirring constantly, until the mixture pulls away from the sides. Cool and make into little balls about 1 inch in diameter. Roll each ball in crystallized sugar. Place in small paper baking cups.
Makes 32 balls.

Coconut and Sweet Potato Balls

(Doce de Batata Doce)

2 cups mashed sweet potatoes
2 cups dried coconut, finely
   grated
1 cup sugar
4 tablespoons chocolate
   powder
1 cup crystallized sugar for
   decoration

*In a medium-sized pan, cook the sweet potatoes, coconut, sugar and chocolate, stirring constantly, until the mixture pulls away from the sides. Cool and make into little balls about 1 inch in diameter and roll in crystallized sugar. Place in small paper baking cups. **Makes 32 balls**.*

Coconut Bars

(Fatias de Coco)

1 cup sugar
2 egg yolks, beaten
1/2 cup unsweetened coconut
   flakes
1/4 cup grated Parmesan
   cheese
1/2 cup powdered sugar
1 teaspoon cinnamon powder

*In a bowl, mix thoroughly the sugar, egg yolks, coconut flakes and Parmesan cheese. Put in a buttered 8x8 inch baking pan and press the mixture flat. Bake in a 350 degree oven for 20 minutes. When slightly cool, cut into small bars and roll in a mixture of powdered sugar and cinnamon. **Makes 9 bars**.*

Coconut Bread Pudding

(Pudim de Pão com Coco)

1/2 cup sugar for caramel
4 slices French bread
2 cups milk
1 cup sugar
2/3 cup coconut milk
1 tablespoon butter or
   margarine, melted
1 cup fine unsweetened
   coconut flakes
5 egg yolks, beaten
1 teaspoon vanilla
3 egg whites, stiffly beaten

In a small heavy pan, melt the sugar over a low temperature until it is caramelized. Pour into a 9 inch diameter ring mold, tilting the pan so that the caramel coats the sides well. In a bowl, soak the bread in the milk and squeeze it through a sieve. Add the sugar, coconut milk, butter, coconut flakes, egg yolks, vanilla and egg whites. Mix well and pour into the mold. Put in a 10x15 inch baking pan containing 1 inch of hot water and bake in a 350 degree oven for 1 hour or until the pudding is set. Let cool. Unmold. **Serves 6.**

Coconut Cake

(Bolo de Coco)

1/2 cup butter or margarine
1 cup sugar
6 eggs, separated
1 cup fine unsweetened
   coconut flakes
1/2 cup coconut milk
2 cups white flour, sifted
1 teaspoon baking powder

In a bowl, beat the butter and sugar until creamy. Add the egg yolks and beat well. Add the coconut flakes, coconut milk, flour and baking powder. Mix thoroughly and fold in stiffly beaten egg whites. Pour into a buttered 9x13 inch baking pan. Bake in a 350 degree oven for 40 minutes or until the cake is done. **Serves 6-8.**

Coconut Custard

(Quindins de Coco)

1 cup sugar
1/2 cup water
2 tablespoons butter or
  margarine, melted
4 tablespoons fresh
  coconut, finely grated
6 egg yolks, beaten
12 custard cups

*In a small pan, combine the sugar and water and cook over a low heat until it spins a thread, stirring occasionally. Add the butter. Cool. Mix the coconut and egg yolks and add to the syrup, stirring well with a wooden spoon. Pour into small, individually buttered custurd cups and put in a 9x13 inch baking pan, containing 1 inch of hot water and bake in a 350 degree oven for 40 minutes. The top of each custard should be light brown in color. Let cool, then place upside down in white paper baking cups. When turned over, the bottom should have a tender, jelly-like consistency. **Makes 10-12.***

Coconut Pudding with Prunes

(Manjar de Coco com Ameixas)

1 cup dried prunes, pitted, chopped
1 cup prune juice
1 cup water
3 cups milk
1 can coconut milk (14 fl. oz.)
1 cup sugar
6 tablespoons cornstarch

In a small pan, cook the prunes, prune juice and water over a low temperature for 10 minutes. Set this sauce aside. In a medium-sized pot, combine the milk, coconut milk, sugar and cornstarch. Bring to a boil, stirring constantly, until thick. Pour into a 9 inch round mold. Put in the refrigerator to chill. When firm, turn the mold upside down on a large platter and tap out the coconut pudding. Pour the prune sauce over it.
Serves 6-8.

Coffee Cake

(Bolo de Café)

1 cup butter or margarine
2 cups brown sugar
4 eggs, separated
2 cups white flour, sifted
1 cup rice flour
1 cup strong coffee
1 teaspoon baking powder

In a bowl, beat the butter and sugar until creamy. Add the egg yolks and beat well. Add all the flour and coffee alternately and mix well. Add the baking powder and fold in stiffly beaten egg whites. Pour into a buttered and floured 9x13 inch baking pan. Bake in a 350 degree oven for 40 minutes or until the cake is done. **Serves 6-8.**

Corn Ice Cream with Coconut Milk

(Sorvete de Milho Verde com Leite de Coco)

3 fresh ears of corn, shucked
1 cup milk
1 can coconut milk (14 fl. oz.)
1 cup sugar
1/8 teaspoon salt
1 yolk, beaten
1 pint whipping cream

Blend the shucked corn with milk until finely minced. Strain this corn milk through a sieve. Discard the residue in the sieve. In a medium-sized pot, bring the corn milk, coconut milk, sugar, salt and yolk to a boil. Cool. When it is completely cool, add the whipping cream and stir well with a wooden spoon. Put the mixture in an ice cream maker or place the mixture in a pan in the freezer and freeze until it is icy and almost set. Scrape it into a mixing bowl and beat it thoroughly with a wooden spoon, or at low speed with an electric mixer. Return it to the freezer and freeze until it is set. **Serves 4-6.**

Cornstarch Butter Cookies
(Biscoitos de Maizena)

1/2 cup butter or margarine
1/2 cup sugar
1/2 cup white flour, sifted
1 cup cornstarch
1 teaspoon vanilla

In a bowl, cream the butter and sugar. Add the flour, cornstarch and vanilla. Mix thoroughly and form into small balls 1 inch in diameter. Put on a buttered cookie sheet. Bake in a 350 degree oven for 20 minutes. **Makes 40 cookies.**

Golden Cake
(Bolo de Ouro)

1/4 cup butter
1/2 cup sugar
4 eggs, separated
1/4 cup milk
1 cup white flour, sifted
1 tablespoon baking powder
1 teaspoon vanilla

In a bowl, beat the butter and sugar until creamy, then add the egg yolks and beat well. Add the milk, flour, baking powder and vanilla and mix well. Stiffly beat the egg whites and gently fold into the mixture. Pour into a buttered 9x13 inch baking pan. Bake in a 350 degree oven for 40 minutes or until the cake is done. **Serves 4-6.**

Grape Tapioca
(Sagú)

1 quart water
1 cup concentrated sweetened
  grape juice
1 cup tapioca pearls
  (not minute tapioca)

In a medium-sized pot, bring the water to a boil. Add the grape juice and the tapioca. Cook uncovered at low temperature, stirring occasionally, for 20 minutes or until the tapioca is clear. Cool before serving. **Serves 6-8.**

Lemon Cake
(Bolo de Limão)

4 tablespoons butter or
  margarine
6 tablespoons sugar
3 eggs, separated
6 tablespoons white flour,
  sifted
1 teaspoon baking powder
1 teaspoon fresh lemon juice
1 teaspoon freshly grated
  lemon peel

In a bowl, beat the butter and sugar until creamy. Add the yolks, flour mixed with baking powder, lemon juice and lemon peel. Mix thoroughly and fold in stiffly beaten egg whites. Pour into a buttered 8x8 inch baking pan. Bake in a 350 degree oven for 40 minutes or until the cake is done. Cool. **Serves 6-8.**

Orange Cake

(Bolo de Laranja)

1/2 cup butter or margarine
1 1/2 cups sugar
1 teaspoon freshly grated
**   orange peel**
3 eggs, separated
2 cups white flour, sifted
1/2 cup fresh orange juice
1 teaspoon baking powder

*In a bowl, beat the butter and sugar until creamy. Add the grated orange peel and egg yolks and beat until well-mixed. Add the flour alternately with orange juice and mix well. Add the baking powder. Mix thoroughly and fold in stiffly beaten egg whites. Pour into a buttered 8x8 inch baking pan. Bake in a 350 degree oven for 40 minutes or until the cake is done. **Serves 6-8.***

Pineapple Upside-down Cake

(Bolo de Abacaxi)

1/4 cup butter or margarine
1/2 cup brown sugar
1 can (20 oz.) sliced pineapple, drained
1 1/3 cups white flour, sifted
1 cup white sugar
3/4 cup milk
1/8 teaspoon salt
1 egg
1 teaspoon baking powder

Heat the butter in a 10-inch ovenproof skillet until the butter is melted. Sprinkle the brown sugar over the butter and arrange pineapple slices on top. Beat remaining ingredients in a large bowl on low speed for 30 seconds, scraping bowl constantly. Beat on high speed for 2 minutes. Pour the mixture over pineapple slices in the skillet, spreading it evenly. Bake in a 350 degree oven for about 40 minutes. Turn the skillet upside down on a large heatproof plate. Let the skillet remain over the cake a few minutes until all the cake and any remaining liquid is out.
Serves 6-8.

Pumpkin Pudding

(Pudim de Abóbora)

1 1/2 cups milk
1/2 cup brown sugar
1/2 teaspoon freshly grated
   orange peel
1/4 teaspoon ground ginger
1 teaspoon ground cinnamon
1/4 teaspoon salt
3 eggs, beaten
1 cup cooked pureed pumpkin

*In a large bowl, combine the milk, sugar, orange peel, ginger, cinnamon and salt. Mix well, then add the beaten eggs and pumpkin. Stir with a wooden spoon until the mixture is smooth, then pour it into a 1-quart, shallow, buttered baking dish. Place the dish in a large baking pan in the middle of the oven and pour enough boiling water into the pan to come halfway up the sides of the baking dish. Preheat the oven at 350 degrees for 5 minutes, then bake for about 1 1/2 hours or until firm. Remove the dish from the water and cool the pudding to room temperature, then refrigerate until thoroughly chilled. **Serves 4-6.***

Rice Cupcake
(Doce de Arroz)

2 eggs, separated
1/2 cup sugar
4 tablespoons butter or
   margarine, melted
1 cup rice flour
1 teaspoon vanilla
1 tablespoon baking powder
muffin tins

*In a bowl, beat the egg whites until stiff. Add the yolks and beat for 3 more minutes. Thoroughly mix in the sugar, melted butter, rice flour, vanilla and baking powder. Pour into small, buttered and floured individual muffin tins and bake in a 350 degree oven for 30 minutes or until the top is browned. **Makes 6.***

Walnut Cake
(Bolo de Nozes)

4 eggs, separated
1 cup sugar
2 tablespoons white flour,
   sifted
2 tablespoons bread crumbs
1 cup ground walnuts

*In a bowl, beat the egg whites until stiff. Add the egg yolks and sugar and beat well. Using a wooden spoon, add the flour, bread crumbs and walnuts and mix well. Pour into a buttered 8x8 inch baking pan. Bake in a 350 degree oven for 30 minutes. **Serves 6-8.***

CHAPTER TEN

DRINKS

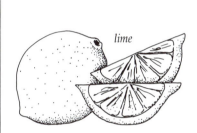

lime

mint

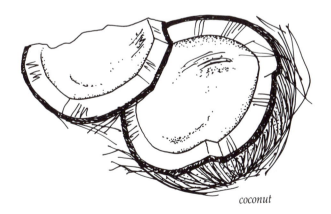

coconut

Drinks

Brazilian Coffee with Milk
(Café com Leite)

1/2 cup ground Brazilian
  coffee
4 cups water
1 pint whipping cream
3 tablespoons sugar

Place a coffee filter in a 6 inch strainer. Put the coffee into the filter and place over a 2 quart pot. Bring the water to a boil and pour over the coffee. Stir the water continuously into the coffee filter. Pour into coffee cups with 1 inch of whipping cream and sweeten according to taste.
Makes 4-6 cups.

Brazilian Hot Chocolate Milk
(Chocolate Quente)

5 cups milk
4 tablespoons sugar
1/2 cup unsweetened cocoa
  powder
1 cup whipping cream

In an uncovered, medium-sized pan, bring the milk and sugar to a boil. Add the cocoa and mix well. Pour into cups and add a large spoonful of whipping cream.
Makes 6 cups.

Cachaça (Brazilian Spirits) Cocktail

(Caipirinha)

2 tablespoons sugar
2 fresh limes, finely grated
   and squeezed
1 cup cachaça or white rum
1 cup crushed ice

*In a small bowl, combine the sugar, grated lime peel and lime juice. Let stand for 5 minutes. Add the cachaça. Pour the cocktail mixture into small glasses filled with ice. **Serves 4.***

Coconut-Cachaça Cocktail

(Batida de Coco)

2 tablespoons freshly grated
   coconut
1 teaspoon sugar
4 cups cachaça or rum
crushed ice

*Mix all the ingredients in a cocktail shaker. Let stand for at least one day in the refrigerator. Serve over crushed ice. **Serves 4-6.***

Strawberry Champagne Punch

(Ponche de Morango)

4 cups champagne
4 cups dry white wine
2 cups strawberries, washed,
  chopped
2 cups soda water
2 tablespoons sugar
2 cups crushed ice

In a large bowl, combine all the ingredients and stir well. Refrigerate before serving.
Serves 12-14.

Strawberry Cocktail

(Coquetel de Morango)

1 cup strawberries, washed,
  drained
3 cups fresh orange juice
1/4 cup whiskey
1 cup crushed ice
3 strawberries, cut in half

Blend the strawberries in the blender until finely minced. Add the orange juice, whiskey and ice and mix well. Place a strawberry half in each glass. Fill with the cocktail mixture.
Serves 6.

Strawberry-Pineapple Punch

(Ponche de Abacaxi)

2 cans (20 oz. each) chunk
  pineapple
4 cups water
2 tablespoons sugar
1 cup dry white wine
1 cup white port wine
2 cups fresh strawberries,
  washed, drained

Blend the pineapple with the water in a blender until finely minced. Strain the pineapple pulp through a sieve into a large bowl. Discard the residue. Add the sugar to the juice and stir well. Cool in the refrigerator. Before serving, add the white wine, port wine and strawberries. Stir well. Chill before serving. **Serves 6-8.**

Shelling and Deveining Shrimp

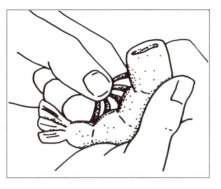

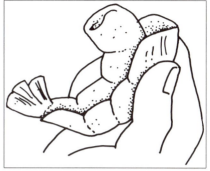

1. From the underside of shrimp, remove the legs.

2. Roll back the shell from the underside, (remove or keep tail, as desired).

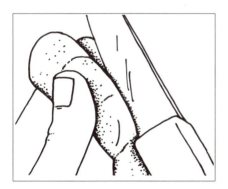

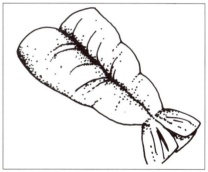

3. To devein, cut along the back (not complettely through) and remove the vein.

4. If butterflying is desired, cut deeper along the back and spread the halves open along the cut in the back.

Cutting and Preparing Stuffed Beef Roll

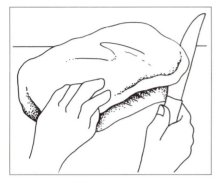

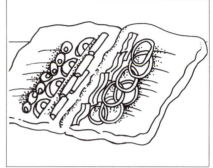

1. Cut the meat down the middle lengthwise so that it opens like a book.

2. Arrange the ingredients in rows and roll the beef tightly.

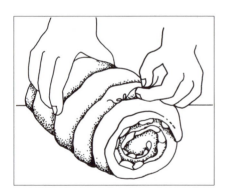

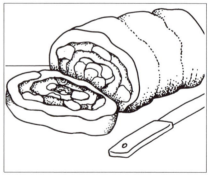

3. Tie the beef with kitchen string after rolling.

4. After cooking, let cool, cut the string, slice the rolled beef, pour the sauce over it and serve.

Suggested Menus

FEIJOADA COMPLETA - Brazilian National Dish

Brazilian Black Beans
Manioc Meal with Butter and Eggs
Brazilian Rice
Collard Greens
Vinaigrette Sauce
Sliced Oranges
Fresh Fruit Juice or Cachaça Cocktail
Fresh Fruit for Dessert
Espresso Coffee

Typical Daily Menu

Brazilian Rice
Beans
Beef with Onions
or
Roast Chicken
Green Leaf Lettuce Salad with Tomatoes
Cooked Vegetable
Condiments
Boiled or Fried Manioc Root
Manioc Meal with Butter and Eggs
Raw or Fried Banana Slices
Fresh Fruit Juice, Soft Drink or Beer
Dessert (one only)
Brazilian Chocolate Nut Squares
Caramel Custard
Coconut and Pineapple Balls
Pumpkin Pudding
Rice Cupcake
Fresh Fruit
Espresso Coffee

Typical Birthday Party for Children

Appetizers

Chicken Balls
Chicken Squares
Cod Fish Croquettes
Deep Fried Bulghar Wheat with Ground Beef and Herbs
Ground Beef Croquettes
Shrimp and Palm Heart Turnovers
Tapioca Bread with Cheese

Sweets

Chocolate Balls
Chocolate Nut Squares
Coconut and Cheese Cupcakes
Coconut and Pineapple Balls
Coconut and Sweet Potato Balls
Coconut Custard
Cornstarch Butter Cookies

Drinks

Fresh Lemonade
Fresh Orange Juice
Guaraná*

Brazilian mothers traditionally serve the birthday treats buffet style. Of course, there is always a birthday cake, several recipes for which can be found in this book.

* Guaraná: The most popular Brazilian soft drink, made from the guaraná fruit, indigenous to the Amazon region of Brazil (Paullinia Cupania).

Essential Ingredients

Bay Leaves

Black Beans

Cachaça

Cashew Nuts

Chayote Squash

Coconut Flakes

Coconut Milk

Corn Meal

Dendê Oil

Dried Cod Fish

Dried Shrimp

Fresh Coriander Leaves

Fresh Limes and Lime Juice

Fresh Mint

Ground Black and White Pepper

Italian Parsley

Malagueta Peppers

Manioc Flour

Manioc Root

Olive Oil

Palm Heart

Parmesan Cheese

Peanuts

Red Vinegar

Tapioca Flour

Vegetable Oil*

*Any kind of oil may be used; however, for better cooking results and for health concerns, I use and recommend the following: for deep-frying, use a refined, high oleic, monounsaturated safflower oil (Spectrum Naturals) or canola oil; for stir-frying, use unrefined, high oleic, monounsaturated safflower oil (Spectrum Naturals) or canola oil. Safflower oil is available in health food stores; canola oil is readily available in supermarkets. In Brazil, peanut oil, corn oil, soya oil, olive oil and palm oil are usually used.

Glossary

Cachaça - Brazilian rum. White rum is a good substitute.

Cayenne Chilies - Very hot chili peppers, available in most markets.

Coconut Milk - Available, canned, in most markets. No substitute.

Coriander - Also known as cilantro and Chinese parsley. Available in most markets. It has a very distinctive flavor. No substitute available.

Dendê - A heavy, yellow-orange palm oil used in Bahian cooking. It has a very rich and unique flavor for which there is no substitute.

Italian Parsley - Broad leafed parsley. Available in most markets.

Malagueta Peppers - Very little, very hot peppers which are difficult to find in the United States. Cayenne peppers are a decent substitute.

Manioc Flour (Cassava Flour) - A fine, grainy flour-like meal, from the pulp of the bitter cassava (or manioc) root. Available in Latino markets. No substitute available.

Manioc Root (also known as Yucca) - A long, brown, irregularly-shaped root with a white starchy interior. Available in Latino and Oriental markets. No substitute available.

Palm Hearts - Tender, ivory-colored hearts or shoots of palm trees which are used as a vegetable or a salad ingredient. Available, canned, in most fancy grade food stores. No substitute available.

Tapioca Flour - Ground cassava root used for desserts and as a thickening agent in cooking. Not minute tapioca. Available in Latino and Oriental markets.

Index

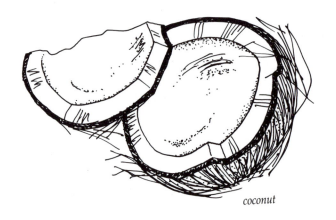

coconut

*Truly **Ambrosia***

Delightful Brazilian Cooking

Delightful Thai Cooking

coming soon

Delightful Italian Cooking

Delightful Tofu Cooking

Ordering Information

Please send me _____ copies of **Delightful Brazilian Cooking** at $14.95 per copy or at $13.95 per copy for 3 or more copies.

           @ $14.95 each
           @ $41.85 for 3 copies $ _____

Shipping & Handling:

           $3.00 1st copy
           $1.50 each additional copy $ _____

Washington State residents, please add
$1.23 for 1 copy, $2.45 for 2 copies,
$3.43 for 3 copies $ _____

                       Total Enclosed $ _____

Payment:

❏ Check   ❏ Money Order

Mail Payment To:

Ambrosia Publications
P.O. Box 30818
Seattle, WA 98103
Phone (206) 789-3693
Fax (206) 789- 3693

Ship Order To:

Name _____
Address _____
City _____
State _____ Zip Code _____

Truly **Ambrosia**

Ordering Information

Please send me _____ copies of **Delightful Thai Cooking** at $10.95 per copy or at $9.95 per copy for 3 or more copies.

        @ $10.95 each
        @ $29.85 for 3 copies $ _____

Shipping & Handling:

        $2.50 1st copy
        $1.50 each additional copy $ _____

Washington State residents, please add
$.90 for 1 copy, $1.80 for 2 copies,
$2.45 for 3 copies $ _____

        Total Enclosed $ _____

Payment:

❏ Check   ❏ Money Order

Mail Payment To:

Ambrosia Publications
P.O. Box 30818
Seattle, WA 98103
Phone (206) 789-3693
Fax (206) 789-3693

Ship Order To:

Name _____
Address _____
City _____
State _____ Zip Code _____